A Chandalini Speaks

ALT *life* voices and stories

AltLife offers stories of individuals, communities and societies. Their voices bear witness to a history, a milieu, an experience, and offer new ways of seeing and understanding our times.

A Chandalini Speaks

Kalyani Thakur Charal

Translated by
Anurima Chanda

Orient BlackSwan

All rights reserved. No part of this book may be (i) modified, reproduced or utilised in any form, or by any means, electronic or mechanical, including photocopying, recording or by any information storage and retrieval system, in any form of binding or cover other than in which it is published, without permission in writing from the publisher; or (ii) used or reproduced in any manner for the purpose of training, development or operation of artificial intelligence (AI) technologies and systems, including generative AI technologies, without permission in writing from the copyright holder.

A CHANDALINI SPEAKS

ORIENT BLACKSWAN PRIVATE LIMITED

Registered Office
3-6-752 Himayatnagar, Hyderabad 500 029, Telangana, India
Email: centraloffice@orientblackswan.com

Other Offices
Bengaluru, Chennai, Guwahati, Hyderabad, Kolkata, Mumbai, New Delhi, Noida, Patna

© Orient Blackswan Private Limited 2026
First published 2026

ISBN 978 93 6973 229 6

Typeset in Cambria 11.5/13.8 *by*
K. Divya, Hyderabad 500 060

041734

Printed at
Manipal Technologies Limited, Manipal

Published by
Orient Blackswan Private Limited
3-6-752, Himayatnagar,
Hyderabad 500 029, Telangana, India
Email: info@orientblackswan.com

Contents

Publisher's Acknowledgements — vii
Introduction/Translator's Note — ix
Interview with Kalyani Thakur Charal — xxiii

1. Yet, Consciousness Evades — 1
2. Problems – Shelter — 9
3. Hostel Samachar — 14
4. Women Development and Guruchand — 19
5. Hyanchra Pujo in the East Bengal Tradition and a Few Wedding Songs — 24
6. The Societal Position of Namashudra Women — 29
7. Matua Philosophy and Today's Politics — 43
8. How Applicable is Western Feminism in a Caste-Divided Society? — 56
9. Dalit Women in Revolutions and Literature — 64
10. A Few Dalit Women in Bengali Literature and Music — 75

Publisher's Acknowledgements

'Yet, Consciousness Evades' translated by Anurima Chanda from the original Bengali 'Tathapi Chaitanya Hoy Na' in *Kalyani Rachana Samagra: Pratham Khondo*, by Kalyani Thakur Charal, Bangla Dalit Sahitya Sangstha, 2021. Used with permission of the publishers

'Problems – Shelter' translated by Anurima Chanda from the original Bengali 'Samasya - Astana' in *Kalyani Rachana Samagra: Pratham Khondo*, by Kalyani Thakur Charal, Bangla Dalit Sahitya Sangstha, 2021. Used with permission of the publishers.

'Hostel Samachar' translated by Anurima Chanda from the original Bengali 'Hostel Samachar' in *Kalyani Rachana Samagra: Pratham Khondo*, by Kalyani Thakur Charal, Bangla Dalit Sahitya Sangstha, 2021. Used with permission of the publishers.

'Women Development and Guruchand' translated by Anurima Chanda from the original Bengali 'Nari Pragati O Guruchand' in *Kalyani Rachana Samagra: Pratham Khondo*, by Kalyani Thakur Charal, Bangla Dalit Sahitya Sangstha, 2021. Used with permission of the publishers.

'Hyanchra Pujo in the East Bengal Tradition and a Few Wedding Songs' translated by Anurima Chanda from the original Bengali 'Purbo Bangiyo Hyanchra Pujo O Kichu Biyer Gaan' in *Kalyani Rachana Samagra: Pratham Khondo*, by Kalyani Thakur Charal, Bangla Dalit Sahitya Sangstha, 2021. Used with permission of the publishers.

'The Societal Position of Namashudra Women' translated by Anurima Chanda from the original Bengali 'Namashudra Meyeder Samajik Obosthan' in *Kalyani Rachana Samagra: Pratham Khondo*, by Kalyani Thakur Charal, Bangla Dalit

Sahitya Sangstha, 2021. Used with permission of the publishers.

'Matua Philosophy and Today's Politics' translated by Anurima Chanda from the original Bengali 'Matua Darshan o Aajker Rajneeti' in *Kalyani Rachana Samagra: Pratham Khondo*, by Kalyani Thakur Charal, Bangla Dalit Sahitya Sangstha, 2021. Used with permission of the publishers.

'How Applicable is Western Feminism in a Caste-Divided Society?' translated by Anurima Chanda from the original Bengali 'Borno-Bibhokto Somaje Poschimi Naaribad Kotota Projojyo' in *Kalyani Rachana Samagra: Pratham Khondo*, by Kalyani Thakur Charal, Bangla Dalit Sahitya Sangstha, 2021. Used with permission of the publishers.

'Dalit Women in Revolutions and Literature' translated by Anurima Chanda from the original Bengali 'Dalit Naari: Sangrame O Sahitye' in *Kalyani Rachana Samagra: Pratham Khondo*, by Kalyani Thakur Charal, Bangla Dalit Sahitya Sangstha, 2021. Used with permission of the publishers.

'A Few Dalit Women in Bengali Literature and Music' translated by Anurima Chanda from the original Bengali 'Bangla Sahitye O Sangeetein Kotipoy Dalit Nari' in *Kalyani Rachana Samagra: Pratham Khondo*, by Kalyani Thakur Charal, Bangla Dalit Sahitya Sangstha, 2021. Used with permission of the publishers.

Introduction/Translator's Note

Within the discourse of caste politics, the case of the 'Dalit woman' assumes a special status. When located within the larger ambit of anti-caste activism, her gendered identity takes a backseat to her caste identity. The Dalit woman's political expression is marginalised and often suppressed. As Anandita Pan has rightly pointed out in the 'Introduction' to *Mapping Dalit Feminism*, 'silence is forced on Dalit women in order to retain the focus exclusively on caste' (1). The blame, however, cannot be solely pinned on the demands of the anti-caste movement at large. Their marginalisation is more complicated and operates at multiple levels. Gopal Guru delineates two factors in tracing the agents of such silencing: 'external factors (non-dalit forces homogenising the issue of dalit women) and internal factors (the patriarchal domination within the dalits)' (2548). Caught between these two forces, the Dalit woman emerges as doubly oppressed—the margin within the margins.

These were the concerns that slowly led to the understanding of the specificity of the Dalit woman's problems and to the emergence of a Dalit feminist consciousness. Various autonomous Dalit women's organisations like the National Federation of Dalit Women (NFDW) and All India Dalit Women's Forum (AIDWF) came up in the 1990s, in order to address these needs in a much more organised manner. While 'underlining the brahmanism of the feminist movement and the patriarchal practices of Dalit politics' (Rege, 'Dalit Women' 39), these organisations specified the need for acknowledging differences within the domain of Dalit feminism. They also took these causes to the international level, creating pressure on local groups to give more weightage to the issues of the Dalit woman—marginalised both by her caste as well as her gender position.

As foregrounded by these groups, intersectionality has emerged as a useful framework within Dalit feminist articulation. It is a methodology that challenges the politics of universalisation by exposing the multifaceted nature of oppression, by exposing the uniqueness of the oppressed group while upholding the differences within. In the case of the Dalit woman, for instance, the lens of intersectionality would serve to throw light on their triply oppressed status (as a Dalit, as a woman, and as a Dalit woman) in the Indian context. This is empowering in its own way as it gives the Dalit woman a separate category to occupy where she can talk about her own issues in her own voice without the fear of being subjugated by her male counterpart—who enjoys a slightly higher position on account of his gender—or her non-Dalit female companions, who occupy a more dominant position in the social ladder. However, this need to separate out their concerns under a different banner might appear divisive to many. Anticipating such allegations, Ruth Manorama has noted how the proponents of such forums emphasise that 'their initiative must not be mistaken for a separatist movement ... [but the] need for strong alliances between the Dalit movement, the women's movement and the Dalit women's movement' while taking into account the individual differences for the realisation of their individual goals. For Dalit women, this goal finds fruition in resisting being silenced as a group and claiming a distinctive identity of their own without being co-opted and appropriated by larger feminist politics as well as Dalit politics, despite sharing solidarities with both.

This is what propels the need among Dalit women to 'talk differently' (Guru 2548), as the representatives of their own reality. Gopal Guru sees this emergence of women's voices as one of the defining features of Dalit feminism. In fact, although institutional articulations on the subject have formed a solid base for the way Dalit feminism has grown over the past two decades, the bulk of the movement has gained from literary writings by Dalit women (Pan 11). Writings by Dalit women, be it autobiographies or other literary formats, have allowed them an important space for identity-making through the opportunity to speak out. Hence, the literature produced by these women has emerged as an important part of their activism.

Evidently, literature plays a dual role when it comes to any marginalised section of society. Apart from its usual literary function, it also becomes a tool for generating awareness and raising a voice of protest. This is the same for Dalit literature. This branch of literature, which gives voice to the margins, has an intensely political core. Whether the political core of this literature supersedes the literary element of these texts, or the literary element cripples the political nature of the text, is another debate. For the present purpose, the intention is to underline how the political and the literary go hand-in-hand in the case of Dalit writing. In fact, it might not be too far-fetched to look upon Dalit literature as acting like a 'catalyst' for Dalit politics, an idea elaborated by Pradeep Kumar Sharma. This literature, which formally began in the 1960s in Maharashtra mainly inspired by Ambedkar (Dangle) and subsequently spread to other parts of India, not only gives literary expression to 'the Dalit movements in India . . . it contributes to shaping those struggles' (Misrahi-Barak et al. 3). In a symbiotic fashion, thus, literature and politics seem to lead each other to forge an alternate historiography of voices that have been silenced so far.

Dalit women's writings also fall under this category of literary production. However, here too, Dalit women face domination from their male counterparts. As Guru notes, 'Dalit male writers do not take serious note of the literary output of Dalit women and tend to be dismissive of it' (2549). Recovering such dismissed narratives and giving them due acknowledgement as alternate sites of knowledge production has been an important step within Dalit feminism. In their articulation of the self, Dalit women's testimonios have been recognised as significant sites of identity-making by laying claim to the authorial agency to tell their own stories. While most of the mapping of Dalit feminism through literature focuses on the mode of autobiographies for textual analysis, there also exists a large body of literary work by Dalit women in various genres that also originate from their lived experiences. These experiences open up windows to a whole new world, narrated in a language that is suited to the cause. In any case, the language of trauma, pain, rage and oppression that is symptomatic of Dalit writings is of a distinct kind, one which can be equated to Rothberg's concept of 'traumatic realism' (55–56). This kind of writing aims at shocking the reader into 'realizing the existence of a world that is vastly and violently different from his/her previous experience' (Pai 76). By experimenting with language and expression, these works thus help develop an alternate vocabulary for Dalit women to speak out against the silencing they have been subjected to throughout the ages.

One such individual who has dedicated her life to this cause is Kalyani Thakur Charal (b. 1965), a Bengali Dalit writer, poet, activist. Her family was forced to migrate to West Bengal following Partition and the family of seven eventually settled down in Bagula around 1954. Followers of the Matua faith and inspired by the teachings of Harichand–Guruchand Thakur, Charal's's father encouraged all his children to acquire an education irrespective of their gender. Charal began writing at the age of eighteen. In the early stages, writing came to her as a form of self-expression almost 'unselfconsciously' as she poured out her poems and short stories into her diary (Gupta 32). With time, as her writings started getting accepted and published in various Bengali little magazines, she gained more confidence in her authorial voice. She went on to self-publish several of her works, and also penned her autobiography *Ami Keno Charal Likhi* (*Why I Sign as Charal*, 2016). She started a vernacular journal titled *Neer*, which means 'nest', urging other women to contribute articles and creative pieces to make their voices heard.

However, before delving into her work against the backdrop of the Dalit feminist movement, it is important to first contextualise her identity as a Bengali Dalit writer. Till about the early twenty-first century, Bengali Dalit literature was relatively unknown as compared to its counterparts from the other regions (Mukherjee 129). One of the main reasons for this, as posited by Sipra Mukherjee, is perhaps 'the severe consequences suffered by the Dalits during the Partition of Bengal, which occurred in 1947' (129). Weakened by the widespread scattering that Partition entailed, the community hardly found any scope, until recently, to find the social and material conditions that are required for any sort of cultural articulation. It is only now that many of these voices have come to the mainstream through the proliferation of scholarship in this area, as well as through works of translation that have brought these writings to the global platform. Charal's voice has emerged among these many voices as a force to reckon with, especially in the domain of Bengali Dalit feminist literature.

The present work attempts to translate her work *Chandalinir Bibriti* (literally meaning 'a Chandalini's statement/account', 2012), a collection of essays, from Bengali to English. So far, all her works that have been translated have been fictional/semi-fictional pieces. This work of non-fiction stands apart from her other works for its chosen genre of articulation—the essay. As a form, essay writing is usually traced back to Plutarch and Seneca, with the birth of the modern essay being credited to Montaigne.

The people who are usually upheld as the greatest essayists of all times are all male (Bloom; Abrams), even though there have been outstanding female essayists who have contributed to the genre. Talking about how the genre was approached by Virginia Woolf, a brilliant essayist herself, Elena Gualtieri writes, 'Her approach to the history and to the nature of the genre was always marked by an attempt to identify within what she saw as a male tradition an alternative line of descent to which she could affiliate herself' (49). Despite this overarching male tradition that is often thrust upon the genre, the essay as a form has been very successfully utilised by women writers and feminist critics 'for their exploration of the intersections between private and public, personal and political' because of its innate nature of being accommodating of 'those deepest rhythms of the kind of personal transformation that is also completely political' (Snyder 171).

Placed against this backdrop, Charal's work emerges as an important text situated within the larger objective of the Dalit feminist movement. She sees her non-fiction as an intricate part of the alternate history-making that has so far been relegated to the margins. She highlights this agenda by noting, 'Since the history of Dalit people has not been written adequately, I feel like it is my responsibility as a Dalit writer to spread awareness among the Dalits through works which penetrate their consciousness much more easily than stories or novels' (this volume xx).

Given that most of these works are written in the writer's native language, translations play a huge role in the dissemination of such works—an essential step for the cause that these books are being written for. While translations of Indian Dalit texts take place both from one Indian language to another as well as into English, the latter assumes prime significance for the wider reach that it guarantees. Talking about the importance of translating Dalit texts, Nalini Pai notes, 'In the context of multilingual and multicultural India, translation into English has become very important in bringing the writing of the marginalized sections of society to the fore' (76). In this context, linguistic transference perhaps comes most easily. The problem arises while translating the context of collective suffering and resistance that is embedded within the language. There is also a general sense of mistrust in this case, especially if the translator identifies as a non-Dalit. Charal talks at length about this at various places, including her interview in this book, pointing out how a greater level of responsibility is expected of such translators and not without reason. These works are not just scattered pieces of literary creation but modes of political resistance and, therefore, in need of informed intervention (Chanda). In this regard, the collaborative translation model (Saha) works wonders, providing a discursive space for all the parties involved in the translation. This technique not only gives the author a chance to remain actively involved in the transference of her text, but also helps the translators fill up the gap that exists between the two knowledge systems—theirs and that of the authors. This is also one of the first steps in challenging power structures, 'for those of us who have been complicit in the power and privileges of caste ... [by realising] our lack of knowledge of cultures that have been violently marginalised' (Rege, "Introduction" 4). Beginning with such understanding of lack creates greater scope for surrendering to the purpose of the text in the Spivakian sense.

In translating these essays, this was one of the prime techniques that I followed—maintaining a constant dialogue with the author. The text being written in prose that is modern and urban did not pose any major challenges in terms of the actual linguistic transference. Similarly, being in the form of an essay, where objective reality comes together with autobiographical elements, there were not many challenges I faced in negotiating with the structure. The problem began with identifying some of the secondary sources that had been used by the author. Since most of the secondary material used by Charal were available to her in translation (for instance, Ambedkar's writings in Bengali as translated from the original English), difficulties were faced in identifying the source text. In cases where the original material was available in English, decisions had to be taken whether to resort to the source text or attempt a back translation of the text into English. This particular issue also posed great difficulties during the process of annotation.

Charal herself noted in one of our personal interactions that she began writing in the essay form when she was not fully aware of the process of proper referencing in writing of this kind. Many of the translations through which she accessed the original essays, were also not adequately annotated. As a result, many of her earlier works lack a proper documentation of the sources she has used in the main text of the essay. This is especially evident in the essays of the first volume, included as the first few essays in this book. For example, in the essay 'Yet, Consciousness Evades', Charal refers to a wide range of secondary sources, starting with the works of philosophers around the world to Indian scriptures. All of them lacked proper citation and had to be used as is. In the same essay, she mentions how even today girls are burnt as sati in Rajasthan. She also refers to another practice called Lausa where women are forced to wear chastity belts by their husbands.[1] In both these cases, the author does not provide sufficient sources. Similarly, in the essay 'Problems – Shelter', Charal refers to the stance of the Health Secretary Lina

---

[1] A report brought out by the Asian Human Rights Commission in 2007, titled 'Chastity belts and other violence against women common in Rajasthan, India', talks in detail about how common this practice is in Rajasthan.

Chakraborty on the subject of inadequate lodging facilities for women. This is used as a stand-alone quote without any sources cited. It was not possible to identify the exact source, as a result of which the quote had to be left without any attribution. There is also a mention of some procession which had been led by street children over the demand for shelter without any adequate reference. Such instances are scattered throughout the text.

Furthermore, many of the essays are also intensely personal, emerging more as opinion pieces. In these essays, the collapse between the private and the public is evident. An example of this could be cited from the essay 'Matua Philosophy and Today's Politics', where Charal questions the sudden rise of interest in the Matuas against the backdrop of the Citizenship (Amendment) Bill (CAB), 2003. The powerful authorial voice cannot be missed as Charal articulates her thoughts on the divided position of the Scheduled Caste refugees of Bengal over the CAB–NRC project. Identifying the role of localised interests as a cause for internal factions within Dalit politics in Bengal, Charal makes some very strong points citing the hunger-strike held by the Matua community against the CAB in Thakurnagar in North 24 Parganas of West Bengal, down to the divided opinion over its 2019 amendment. She mentions how the larger politics of Bengali Dalits got derailed when the leaders at the forefront decided to settle for crumbs.

Her criticisms of the leadership all arise out of her own engagements with politics at the ground level and are rooted in the political emerging out of the personal. Although most of this information also lies scattered in various print and online media, a more extensive syncing of both could have further fortified the criticism, especially for readers unfamiliar with the terrain. As a translator, this gap could have been adjusted through the use of annotations lying beyond the authorial voice. However, a decision was taken to leave it as it is for the purpose of the current project, as it seemed more appropriate to leave the authorial intent untarnished and open to readerly interpretation. This was also aligned with my vision as a translator of a project of the present kind, where the intention was in capturing the female subjective position towards alternate meaning-making in the understanding of a social situation leading up to its critical decoding. In a world where men continue to dominate op-ed and editorial pages in mainstream newspapers (Agarwal; Solomon; Tarpley), owing largely to fewer contributions by women who continue to discount their knowledge, it appears important to let these voices speak for themselves without being restricted by the need to fit into stringent structures laid down by academia—another world dominated by men.

This collection also hosts essays that look at indigenous traditions like that of the Hyanchra pujo, Shubhochandi pujo, Sankranti preparations in rural Bengal, et cetera. Many of the items listed in relation to these traditions, like the different kinds of pithe/sweetmeats, or embroidery styles, or woven mattresses, or ghute/dung-fuel et cetera., are region–culture-specific with no easy equivalences. These have been retained in the original with footnotes where necessary. The documented songs or extracts from hagiographies used in the essays also fall under this category. Being in the local dialect or in verse-form, they proved tricky during their transference to the target culture in the same format. For example, let's take the first verse from the essay 'Hyanchra Pujo in the East Bengal Tradition and a Few Wedding Songs':

Hyanchra Thairon lo tor
Fyaachra chul
Taaite baindhye debo
Lohagoraar phul
Lohagoraar phul na
Bennaar maati
Amager baap-bhai surjo shonaar kaathi.

Here, the devotee is addressing the Hyanchra Thairon or 'thakurani' (referring to the goddess). Even though the verse is not in standard Bengali, the meaning of the words are decipherable in general. The problem arises while trying to translate local references like 'lohagorer phul' or 'bennaar maati'. The word 'fyaachra' too was new for me. Hence, authorial inputs were crucial here. Charal pointed out that 'fyaachra' denotes 'elo kesh' (dishevelled hair) and 'lohagorer phul' is a kind of wild flower. However, she was not able to decipher the meaning of 'benna' from 'bennaar maati'. Although she mentioned that the word usually stands for 'reri-r tel' or castor oil, she was not able to decode the exact usage here. In the absence of the exact meaning, it was difficult to translate the verse. In this case, therefore, the issue was resolved by adding a footnote elucidating the meaning of the song. The same technique has been used for all the songs in the essay.

For the verse-extracts used in essays like 'Yet, Consciousness Evades' or 'Women's Development and Guruchand', loose translations were attempted. Most of these extracts, taken from Matua hagiographies which were composed in the oral panchali and mangalkavya traditions using payar chhanda (a rhyming couplet form), pose challenges in terms of transferring the exact rhyme and rhythm from Bengali to English. Choices were made according to each individual case. For instance, the two verse-extracts 'Prabhu sabe bole daki' and 'Ei bhabe biyaa hoy' (both taken from Mahananda Haldar's *Sri Sri Guruchand Charit*) in 'Yet, Consciousness Evades' were translated using different rhyme schemes despite being from the same text. These were further supplemented with paraphrases in footnotes. For other essays using similar verse-extracts, like 'The Societal Position of Namashudra Women', 'Matua Philosophy and Today's Politics', and 'A Few Dalit Women in Bengali Literature and Music', only the paraphrased content was provided through footnotes.

The entire process of translation, however, took me longer than expected as I also needed to distance myself from the work periodically before returning to it. As I have realised over time, pauses are as important as active engagement in translations of this kind which aim to serve larger purposes, as it gives one the chance to separate their emotional response to these texts from their objective response. The text as it stands today, is a product of such engagements, disengagements, revisitations, critical introspections and editorial suggestions. I hope I have been able to do justice to the cause and also been able to bring out the language/context of difference that the original aspires towards.

I am thankful to Kalyani-di for trusting me with her words and to Jaydeep Sarangi for directing me to this work. My deepest gratitude to Mukti Chanda, Sipra Mukherjee, Sohini Gupta, Kanad Sinha, and Arpita Pandey for tirelessly helping me track down obscure references, making the verification process much easier. I am also grateful to Sreenath Sreedharan from Orient BlackSwan for his immense patience in allowing me to work at my own pace despite several missed deadlines. A heartfelt thanks to Namrata Kartik for the handholding during the crucial editing phase, and to Mahalakshmi Jayaram for spotting some significant (and some rather silly) errors in my translation that could have led to major inaccuracies.

References

Abrams, M. H. "Essay". *A Glossary of Literary Terms*. Heinle & Heinle, 1999, p. 82.

Agarwal, Cherry. "An anatomy of op-ed and editorial pages". *Newslaundry*, 4 February 2019, https://www.newslaundry.com/2019/02/04/an-anatomy-of-op-ed-and-editorial-pages. Accessed 30 May 2023.

Bloom, Harold. *Essayists and Prophets*. Chelsea House Publishers, 2005.

Chanda, Anurima. "How to Translate Trauma and Rage? My Experiences as a Translator of a Dalit Text". *Negotiations: An International Journal of Literary and Cultural Studies*, vol. 4, 2021, pp. 101–10.

Dangle, Arjun, editor. *Poisoned Bread: Translations from Marathi Dalit Literature*. Orient BlackSwan, 2009.

Gualtieri, Elena. *Virginia Woolf's Essays: Sketching the Past*. Palgrave Macmillan, 2000.

Gupta, Jayati. "Kalyani Thakur Charal". *Dalit Text; Aesthetics and Politics Re-Imagined*, edited by Judith Misrahi-Barak, et al., Routledge, 2019, pp. 30–43.

Guru, Gopal. "Dalit Women Talk Differently". *Economic and Political Weekly*, 14–21 Oct. 1995, vol. 30, no. 41/42. pp. 2548–550.

Manorama, Ruth. "Background Information on Dalit Women in India". *Women's UN Report Network*, https://wunrn.com/2006/12/india-dalit-women-in-india/. Accessed 5 June 2023.

Mukherjee, Sipra. "Creating their Own Gods: Literature from the Margins of Bengal". *Dalit Literatures in India*, edited by Joshil K. Abraham, and Judith Misrahi-Barak, Routledge, 2016, pp. 128–42.

Pai, Nalini. "Language and Translation in Dalit Literature". *Dalit Literatures in India*, edited by Joshil K. Abraham and Judith Misrahi-Barak, Routledge, 2016, pp. 76–92.

Pan, Anandita. *Mapping Dalit Feminism: Towards an Intersectional Standpoint*. Sage and Stree, 2021.

Rege, Sharmila. "Dalit Women Talk Differently: A Critique of 'Difference' and Towards a Dalit Feminist Standpoint Position". *Economic and Political Weekly*, vol. 33, no. 44, 31 October 1998, pp. WS39–46.

---. Introduction. *Writing Caste/Writing Gender: Reading Dalit Women's Testimonios*. Zubaan, 2006, pp. 1–8.

Rothberg, Michael. "Between the Extreme and the Everyday: Ruth Kluger's Traumatic Realism". *Extremities: Trauma, Testimony and Community*, edited by K. Nancy Miller, and Jason Tougaw, U of Illinois P, 2002.

Saha, Saswati. "Discoursing Translation as an act of Collaboration: An Indian approach". Students' Workshop on Translation, 26 May 2003, Department of English, University of North Bengal, Siliguri. Lecture.

Sharma, Pradeep Kumar. *Dalit Literature and Politics*. Shipra Publications, 2006.

Snyder, John. *Prospects of Power: Tragedy, Satire, the Essay and the Theory of Genre*. UP of Kentucky, 1991.

Solomon, Maddie. "Op-ed writing wants to keep marginalized voices out. Let's change that". *Women's Media Centre*, 06 Nov. 2019, https://womensmediacenter.com/fbomb/op-ed-writing-wants-to-keep-marginalized-voices-out-lets-change-that, accessed 30 May 2023.

Tarpley, Mallary Tenore. "Why women don't contribute to opinion pages as often as men & what we can do about it". *Poynter*, 25 Feb. 2011, https://www.poynter.org/reporting-editing/2011/why-women-dont-contribute-to-opinion-pages-as-often-as-men-what-we-can-do-about-it/. Accessed 30 May 2023.

Interview with Kalyani Thakur Charal

Q: What makes Dalit writing from West Bengal different from other parts of India?

Dalit literature of West Bengal is very different from other places because the ragging here is more scientific ragging,[1] which is not as clearly evident as in other parts of the country. Hence, its reflection in literature is also quite different. Here, caste hegemony is the reason behind Chuni Kotal committing suicide, Maroona Murmu becoming a victim of violent online trolling, or Saraswati Kerketta being subjected to harassment along caste-lines from her colleagues.[2] If we look at Matua literature, at texts like

---

[1] Charal's use of the colloquial 'scientific ragging' points to the fact that caste discrimination in West Bengal operates subtly—she uses the Bengali word 'sukkho'—often disguised, unlike the overt violence seen in other states. Despite Bengal's reputation of being 'casteless' (see Meenakshi Mukherjee's essay referred to in the 'Introduction'), the existence of ancient texts and hagiographies referencing caste suggests otherwise. Charal argues that Bengal's caste dynamics involve a more 'subtle (caste-based) ragging', creating an illusion of caste absence. This subtle oppression is reflected in the phrase 'hathe marbe na, bhaate marbe' (they won't hit you directly, but they'll cut off your source of livelihood, like food/rice), symbolising a method of incapacitating someone without overt violence, yet with equally damaging consequences.

[2] Chuni Kotal, a Dalit Adivasi of the Lodha Shabar tribe, became the first woman graduate from the tribe in 1985. Her death through suicide on 16 August 1992 followed years of harassment by officials. Maroona Murmu, from the Santhal community, is an Associate Professor at Jadavpur University's history department. She has faced casteist trolling on Facebook, has been accused of being incompetent, and faced widespread discrimination in

Sri Sri Harililamrito and *Sri Sri Guruchand Charit*, we will get a clear picture of the caste system of Bengal. The issues of untouchability and the rise of the Matua religion as a response against it, clearly emerges in Matua literature. There is no mention of these books in the history of Bengal or Bengali literature. This proves how much the gentlemen here cherish literature that we do not even find the mention of any such works in their literature. Biographies of great men are not mentioned in history because of the writer's pride in their high-caste status. Their history has been erased from Bengali literature, from the history of Bengal. Dalit literature was born with the urge to write a new history.

Q: Within this larger category of Dalit writing, where can we situate Dalit women's writing?

Dalit girls, tribal girls, and girls from the minority sections of society, are educationally and economically far behind as compared to girls from other sections of society. There are a lot of obstacles in the way to Dalit literature, where the authors, publishers and sellers are all Dalit writers themselves. It is very difficult for a Dalit woman writer to transcend that barrier. Moreover, Dalit literature is not literature for pleasure because of which its subject matter and style of writing are very different. Dalit girls still haven't progressed to the level of education that is required to contribute to Dalit literature. Hence, one can find only a handful of Dalit women writers. They need more educational and economic opportunities along with awareness about Dalit issues. Dalit female writers very obviously have different ideas than feminist writers because they are much

---

academia because she belongs to a Scheduled Tribe. Saraswati Kerketta, Head of the Department of Geography, Rabindra Bharati University, was physically and emotionally harassed using her caste, skin tone, birthplace, and gender.

further behind in generational education than the latter. As much as they need more opportunities to progress further, they also need more time.

Q: Where can we place Dalit women's writings vis-à-vis women's writing in India?

The difference between Dalit women's writing and Indian women's writing in general is that there are very few women writers whose works are specifically focused on Dalits, the caste system, the role of religion, the history of social thinkers from the lower echelons of life, et cetera. With regard to the Dalit women writers, the ones who are writing today face a lot of obstacles in the path of their work. All of them have to cross these hurdles to write about eminent figures who have been branded as untouchables and not given a place in history despite their immense social contribution. Their work is committed to bringing such marginalised voices to the forefront through their writings, along with writing about Dalit subjugation and the ways of overcoming it. Since most of them acquired education much later than their upper-caste counterparts, we only get to hear a limited number of such Dalit women writers. Among non-Dalits, we may find a handful of women writers like Kalyani Bandopadhyay, Sukumari Bhattacharya and Devi Chattopadhyay who write about Dalit issues, about caste, class and religious divisions. But apart from them, no other women writers from the country have written consistently on these issues or even on Ambedkar, especially from a region like Bengal. Therefore, Dalit women have been trying to fill in these gaps by addressing such issues in their works, though to a lesser extent. The attempt is to restore the dignity of those that are left out of history with the hope that others too will realise their importance.

Q: As a writer, do you write with the consciousness of a Dalit 'woman' writer or simply a Dalit writer?

I am a Dalit writer as well as a Dalit woman writer. This is because the patriarchy which I experience within our social system as a woman in general, exists within Dalit society too. However, many great men took birth within Dalit society who took up the cause of women's advancement and spoke boldly in favour of women's freedom. These include, Harichand–Guruchand Thakur, Jyotirao Phule, Periyar E. V. Ramasamy, and above all Babasaheb Dr B. R. Ambedkar. My father was also very liberal and modern-minded on the subject of women's freedom and equal rights for children irrespective of their gender. A Dalit woman is doubly oppressed: one, due to the patriarchal social structure, and the other due to the caste-based social structure.

Q: Why is it important to assert this female identity? Does the larger politics of Dalit identity cause a silencing of the Dalit women's identity?

This is important not just to assert. I feel that when we talk about caste, the issue of gender comes up for very natural reasons. In the feminist movement, it is seen that the voice of the Dalit girl is suppressed by the writings or speeches of upper-caste or privileged women. Dalit women's writing is important in bringing back that voice to the surface. Social wounds will fester if they are ignored. Therefore, Dalit women need to be allowed to speak for themselves. The feminist movement is, perhaps, more to blame for suppressing Dalit women's voices than Dalit politics. I feel that almost 85 per cent of society needs women's voices and their political presence, not neglect or indifference.

Q: When did you start writing?

Just like many other boys and girls from Bengal, I started writing at the age of 18–20, beginning with romantic poetry. At that time, I used to put down all my writing in a diary.

Q: What are your primary goals as a Dalit woman activist/writer?

Obviously, to see the participation of Dalit people and women in all fields, such as education, politics, health, economy, in direct proportion to their numbers. This is something that is absolutely desirable from any developed society or a strong state.

Q: Why did you decide to add the word 'Charal' to your pen-name?

I have had to face a lot of questions because of my surname, Thakur. This is mainly because the surname Thakur is usually a high-caste surname. If I use my caste identity in my pen-name, I wouldn't need to explain it anymore. Apart from this, it is also my form of protest against the gentleman-class who use the words 'charal', 'chamar' very loosely with neglect, as everyday insults. You can say that I use it as a slap on the faces of these gentlemen, so that they dare not treat any other community as poorly as they wish in future. Moreover, I used to edit a little magazine while employed in a government job, which is legally not allowed. So, it seemed at one point of time that something else must be added to the name. Articulating my identity became easier. The Dalit literary movement is in a sense the struggle for identity. I have had to hear verbal slurs from the mouths of my colleagues at a workplace where I have faced many adversities. Some of it is mentioned in my autobiography. You all know that the upper-caste people abuse the Chandalas as Charals. I use this word to shame them.

Q: You usually write poems. What made you write essays?

Personally, I love reading both poetry and essays. I guess that is the reason I started writing essays. I have observed that among the Dalits who wish to read a different kind of literature, they prefer to read their own history, political history, or the lives of great personalities, over stories or novels. Since the history of Dalit people has not been written adequately, I feel like it is my responsibility as a Dalit writer to spread awareness among Dalits through works which penetrate their consciousness much more easily than stories or novels. Poems come from emotions. In them, love, anger, reaction to social injustice emerges effortlessly in the writing. To write essays, one needs to read certain books which are important, like books on feminism or Ambedkar's writings, which are not easily available. I ask others also to write essays. It will not only bring out their thoughts and ideas, but is also necessary for the cause.

Q: Why did you decide to title the volume of essays *Chandalinir Bibriti*?

After my book of verse *Chandalinir Kobita* (*Poems by a Chandalini*) was published, a renowned poet and activist wrote a review of the book for a little magazine, *Chetana Lahar*. In the beginning of the review, he praised me, but it turned out to be fake as right at the end he mentioned that none of my poems sounded like poems, but were rather like bibriti ('statements'). The essays that eventually went into this book had already been written much before. I had not yet decided the title of the book. The following year, I published the book of essays and borrowed his phrase for the title. I even informed the poet that my book of essays was out and that I had titled it *Chandalinir Bibriti*. Many of the essays in the book, however, are lectures I have delivered at various events.

Q: Could a non-Dalit have expressed the angst of a Chandalini as well as a Dalit writer?

This is perhaps not possible. The two words 'sympathy' and 'empathy' will explain the difference. One is Dalit literature and the other, literature written in sympathy with the Dalits.

Q: What are your views about the translation of Dalit texts?

Dalit literature gains a larger audience through translations. Moreover, there is no other alternative way to get acquainted with the writings of Dalit writers in different languages except through translation. There are so many people living in our country, there should be one common medium. Especially, with English translation, the texts get an opportunity to reach a large number of people within the country and outside, and brings about the scope for a greater exchange of ideas.

Q: How are translating Dalit texts different from other texts? Is there an added responsibility?

There are a lot of regionalisms or the usage of regional words in Dalit literature. Till now, most of the people translating these works are not familiar with most of these words. Given this case, the translations have a lot of issues. If the translator is from that particular region or community, then chances are that there will be a more faithful translation and justice will be done to the work. Some responsibility always exists.

Q: Often there is a lot of mistrust generated when a non-Dalit translator translates a Dalit text. How can such mistrust be negotiated?

There are also good reasons for this mistrust. Some translators (not all) have translated erroneously, using words that could dangerously change the meaning of the text. These books have also been printed and published. A simple way to solve this problem is to translate in workshops where the author too will be present. Not everyone is supposed to know the words of all the regions.

Therefore, I think that if you sit with the author or find out the meaning of the word from the author, there will be no problem with the translation.

Q: Do you write for a particular kind of audience?

This is true in part, if not completely. However, our job also entails spreading awareness among all kinds of people. While it is important to spread Dalit awareness, to rid the society of caste hatred is also a part of our job. The people of a certain section of society should be made to understand that caste hatred is a heinous crime and a type of injustice. They should also be made aware that we need to be freed from this brahminical and Manuvadi mentality.

Q: Do you think that Dalit women's writing has reached the mainstream or is there more to be done?

Publishers of every province should come forward to publish Dalit literature, especially the works of Dalit women. Only then will the so-called mainstream literature reach all the readers. There are already some people who are interested in this kind of writing. New topics are coming from the pens of many Dalit girls, which we publish in our magazine *Neer Ritupatra*. Before this, hardly any women writers were to be found in the area of Bengali literature. Women writers from the so-called mainstream haven't written on the lives of Ambedkar, Phule, Periyar, Harichand–Guruchand. Why won't the Dalit girls, from a place of social responsibility, take up their pens? And why will only men write? Girls will need to be more educated and aware, and will also have to take up thoughtful writing along with creative writing. If a section of the society is still backward, that society cannot be referred to as a developed society, just as that country cannot be called a developed country.

1
Yet, Consciousness Evades

First published in 1993 in Satyer Sandhane *('Search for Truth'), souvenir volume published at the Bagula Matua Conference*

Different philosophers from different parts of the world have presented different opinions on God. According to the Greek philosopher Plato, God is the 'Idea of Good' or what you may call a good sense. Aristotle opines that God is the 'Prime Mover' of the world. Plotinus believes God is the one and only, the infinite and the eternal. One can perceive God through one's transcendental senses. Hegel is of the view that God is the seat of ultimate wisdom. These notions of God reveal their presence through the inanimate world, the heart, and society in different dimensions. This higher power is one among many; the unity among diversity. For Schelling, God is a neutral supreme being, beyond the knower and knowledge. According to Fichte, God is the 'Absolute Ego' who has no temporal presence.

In Indian philosophy, however, the soul or the higher soul has been presented as the essence of being. In the *Aitareya Upanishad* we find:

> purushe ha vaa ayamaadito garbho bhavati yadetadretaha
> tadetatsarvebhyongebhyastejaha
> sambhootamaatmanyevaatmaanam bibharti

tadyadaa striyaam sinchatyathainajjanayati tadasya prathaman janma (chapter 2, verse 1)

That is, the semen is born in the body of a man from the worldly soul. This semen draws vigour from the rest of the body and channels it to the woman. That is how it gives birth to itself. This becomes the first birth. In this case only the semen has been shown as the form of soul, even though science says that an embryo is created as a result of the union of the sperm and the egg. In this context, the soul is depicted as singular in focus, carried forward through the male child into the next generation.

The distinguished Indian philosopher, Deviprasad Chattopadhyay, has mentioned in an interview how *Charak Samhita* is the chief text that lies at the core of Indian science. Stating that the scientific side of *Charak Samhita* has been suppressed by the casteist organisation of society, Chattopadhyay holds that those who want a society that is dictated by religious texts have attempted to infiltrate the minds of people with certain ideologies. Instead, the ideology one must depend on to sustain a society—one which conforms to a religious code—is 'work'. If the doctrine of 'do your own work' is practised, the entire discipline of medicine will become obsolete.

This is similar to how people accepted the opinion of Galileo almost three-hundred-and-fifty years after his death. However, he had to tolerate inhuman torture till the end of his life over his heliocentric theory. Giordano Bruno was burnt to death for the same sin. His fault was that he had said, 'God is revered on countless suns, not one. His glory is not just limited to earth but thousands of other planets.'

Plato and Hegel's definitions of God taken together is considered to be the most logical in today's situation, whereby 'God' means 'good sense'; an idea which creates unity among differences.

Although in Indian philosophy the soul is shown as male, around the twelfth to tenth or ninth century BCE, that is during the composition of the *Rig Veda*, the place of women was at the top. In the words of Dr Sukumari Bhattacharya, 'At the end of the Vedic period, there were many foreign invasions. As a result, women were pushed into the hinterlands due to the fear of female abduction and interbreeding, and from then on, women became more vulnerable. In other words, shudras and women have had to pay the price for any problem inside or outside the house.'

The status of women was the same not only in the East but also in the West. August Bebel has written how in the first century CE, many strong but uneducated groups joined the weak Roman Empire and emerged victorious by opposing the strict practices of Christianity. These groups of people operated on principles very different from the Romans. Tacitus admits that they were the only barbarous races who were content to take only one wife. If any of their wives committed adultery, her husband would shave her head, strip her naked, and drive her out of the village in front of her relatives. In this case adulterous women were punished, not adulterous men.

Germany, like all other ancient nations, also had a patriarchal society. There, relatives would gift the family two loads of wood if a son was born to them, but only one load of wood if a daughter was born. From this it can be seen that they valued a daughter at half the price of a son.

This was the situation in the first century CE, which goes back almost two thousand years. Coming back to the present age, in this country itself, a more horrible and barbaric practice known as Lausa is still prevalent in Rajasthan, where girls are burnt as sati to this date. There, to preserve the woman's chastity, their husbands make them wear an iron undergarment and keep it locked, withholding the key for themselves. This is to ensure that the wife does not commit adultery in the absence of the husband.

It appears that throughout the ages, the subject of abstinence has always been considered as the woman's department. And pleasure? Men have been given exclusive rights to that. Even though abstinence suppresses disorder, it is also contrary to our innate nature. This is because the body seeks sexual pleasure just like its other urges. Going against nature causes various neurological and mental diseases.

The social image of any era is found in the literature of that age, as literature is the reflection of society. As it happens, all ancient Indian literature was written by men. And women? They were not even allowed to read scriptures, just like the shudras. So both of them fell behind.

Later, the person who led these marginalised people forward was Guruchand Thakur, one of the world's most radiant and enlightened minds. His unwavering character and foresight contributed to the welfare of the community. Perhaps, before any vulnerable group faces extinction, such a leader emerges to guide them. At a time when a powerful class in Bengal was on the verge of collapse, he showed the light to the illiterate and weak sections of society. This backward group was physically strong but unaware about the benefits of education. Their origin story, whether they had descended from Aryans or non-Aryans, remains a highly debated topic. Whatever be their identity—as shudras, Namos, Chanrals, Chandalas, and so on—Guruchand Thakur, with the help of the British Government, helped them register themselves as 'Namashudras'.

There are two types of shudras mentioned in literature: the slaves and the wage-earners. All shudras are not slaves. Among the wage-earners are Brishols, Pushkosh, Swapaks, Dombas and Chandalas. Even though in the *Sri Sri Guruchand Charit*, Mahananda Haldar (the author) has shown a difference between the Chandalas and the Namashudras, it is best not to get into such debatable issues but focus on whether it was that important to change the name from Chandala or Chanral. In whatever name they may be registered, be it Namashudra or Chandala, the main purpose was their educational progress.

The act of changing one's name is a sign of inferiority. Maybe the social environment of that era propelled this. In this case, women were used as a means of exchange. In these negotiations, Chandala became Namashudra in exchange for the acceptance of widow remarriage. Although Guruchand Thakur was opposed to child marriage and polygamy, he did not fully approve of widow remarriage, as can be gathered from these lines:

Prabhu shobe bole daki	*aro kotha ache baki*
The lord calls all	with more to say
Ei karjo bohu na koribe.	
Not many this way will act.	
Udyesshyo puron hole	*ei karjo kono kale*
If cause is served	at any given age
Kora nahi juktijukto hobe?	
What logic will support this fact?	
Onachari byabhichari	*aache joto noronari*
Fornicators, adulterers, and men	all those women
Ei korme paiye sujog	
will seize the opportunity.	
Matuar neeti ei	*bidhobar biye nei,*
States Matua law	no marriage for widows,
Baalyo bibaaher koro bondho.	
Rather child marriages dismiss.	
Bidhoba pabitra bhabe	*jibone bachiya robe*
Pure the widows will this way,	living their lives stay

6 A Chandalini Speaks

Poro jonme dur hobe mondo.
washing away their sins in the next. (251)¹

Alas, the afterlife! In this life, the one who is being granted the mere right to exist—what about their afterlife? If a widow has an afterlife, then why doesn't a widower? The scriptures have not imposed any restrictions on him. An adulteress cannot exist alone; there must also be a man. And marriage is a social recognition—so where does the question of adultery arise in that case? Even though that recognition is akin to a burning pyre, a sacrificial slaughter.

It has recently been revealed in the news that the application of Catholic girls from the US to become priests has been rejected. A five-member committee made up of US Roman Catholic bishops have said that according to the Vatican's rules, God wants only men to be his priests. We, ourselves, don't know what our gods want.

Sri Sri Guruchand Charit further says,

Ei bhabe biyaa hoy koy	*probhu debi chande*
Aar nahi kore proyojon	
Jaahaa holo ei bhalo	*e jaati uddhaar holo*
Aar biyaa dibo ki karon? (25)²	

---

¹ The Lord calls out to everyone to express his desire to say some more on the topic. He says that widow remarriage can never be allowed as it will provide lawless adulterers with more advantages. The Matua rules do not allow widow remarriage, but child marriage must be stopped. Widows should lead a pure life so that their sorrows vanish in the next life.

² Guruchand Thakur, the Lord, tells his disciple Debichand how widow remarriages started and uplifted the caste group. But now that their purpose has been served, why should the process continue? The passage questions the need for widow remarriage, suggesting that it was initially implemented for social upliftment but is no longer necessary. It reflects a shift and implies that now that the community has already been saved, there is no longer a reason to maintain the practice.

The need for widow remarriage arose only to make the Chandalas into Namashudras. As soon as the mission was accomplished, widows were pushed back to their previous state of existence. What would have been the societal harm if the Namashudras had remained Chandalas, and how did widows benefit by changing their name from Chandalas to Namashudras? Women have always been exploited. Through eternity, they have always been used for the benefit of society, for the benefit of men. Still, foolish as they are, women unquestioningly continue to obey the rules set down by the scriptures. They never even turn the pages and realise that everything in the scriptures is against them.

And restraint? It comes from human values. If it is forced, the result will always be the opposite. In view of the growing population, humans naturally become eager to practice restraint. For this, education is a necessity. Human values are inculcated through the building of one's character, usually conferred upon the individual by the family. To build a civilised, beautiful, innovative, healthy society, one has to first personally develop themselves and their family, because ultimately it is the individual who is the origin of the collective.

The purpose of the above statement is not to create division between men and women or to disrupt the peace of the world. Men and women complement each other. They will continue to coexist naturally. But that coexistence should be accompanied by respect for each other. To create a sense of alliance between both the sexes, it is necessary to abandon certain age-old ideas with a liberal mind, or else it will be impossible to keep pace with the present progressive society. Instead of treating her like a second-class citizen as soon as she is born, the attempt should be to at least treat the girl-child as equal to a boy-child. The idea that the girl-child will be the end of the family lineage should be abandoned. A child of any gender, of any creature, is the carrier and bearer of its lineage. The desire for a son right after having a daughter not only increases the population, but is a humiliation of femininity. Instead of treating the girl-child as a burden and discarding her in someone else's house, if our fathers make sure that their daughters can independently provide for themselves like any son, there will be some redemption for this dying breed. Instead of making them play with dolls and dollhouses, the attempt should be to provide them the education that will help them take ownership of their future independently. It will not only be good for the girl, but also for society.

Our semi-scientific and semi-philosophical attitude is responsible for female infanticide today. Scientific sonography is helping us determine the sex of the foetus before it is born and, guided by the rotten, age-old belief that a family is doomed without a son, we are committing foeticide. When religion becomes a cultural hangup, it not only burns people but also sets fire to temples and mosques. 'Good sense', after banging its head against these walls, returns, only to see from afar how deep the divides between people have become. Yet, consciousness evades us!

2
Problems – Shelter[1]

Published in Neer Ritupatra, *2nd Issue, 1995.*

To escape natural disasters, nomadic human groups started building shelters from trees and branches. With the progress of civilisation, the raw materials used for building shelters changed. From grass and foliage to straw, mud, wood, tin, and eventually to brick, brick-dust, wood, lime and cement. With time, cracks began appearing within these groups too. People from the same bloodline started segregating themselves into families and in due course nuclear families came into existence. The husband, the wife, and the child. Problems arose when, owing to financial constraints, both the husband and the wife were forced to leave their homes and spend a considerable part of their day outside. As a result, the child had to be left in a crèche or a hostel. In this fashion, the nuclear family setup also started disintegrating. Thus began the proliferation of solo living. Not just children; today the young, the old, and many others are victims of a lonely life with a crisis of security. Their chief concern is shelter.

---

[1] The people quoted in this chapter were interviewed by the author in the course of her research for this essay.

Various natural and social disasters have often led humans to destitution. Because of wars, riots, epidemics, famines and floods, the refugee crisis continues to exist. The problems that surfaced because of wars or Partition are still visible. Much before Partition, people from the villages had started migrating to cities due to educational and professional demands. This prompted the need for lodging. Boarding houses (popularly known as 'mess-baris' in Bengal) started cropping up throughout cities. Certain parts of cities bear evidence of this fact even today. Even some cinema[2] from the sixties bears testimony to this peculiar phenomenon. Many of today's artists and litterateurs[3] have also lived a portion of their lives in these mess-baris.

With time, there was a rise in female literacy. Therefore, hostels for women started coming up in areas adjacent to educational institutions. Today, this has become an acute problem. For working individuals living alone, both men and women, the necessity of a hostel or boarding is paramount. What is surprising is the fact that these people don't have any separate association of their own. Even street hawkers, tenants, rickshaw-pullers have associations—but hostel boarders not only lack an association, they are also not as vocal about their problems. It is because of this that boarders have to face various issues, including ragging. Orphan girls are disappearing from these homes. Residents of orphanages are being forced to commit suicide because of inhuman torture. The unscrupulous owners of private

---

[2] The Bengali comedy film *Shaarey Chuattor* (1953), considered to be a classic, is based on such a mess-bari. The film was directed by Nirmal Dey.
[3] Literary stalwarts from Bengal like Sharatchandra Chattopadhyay, Saradindu Bandyopadhay, Bibhutibhusan Bandyopadhyay, Jibananda Das and others, have lived in such mess-baris. The fictional detective-figure Byomkesh Bakshi, created by Saradindu Bandyopadhyay, begins his career from a mess-bari in the story 'Satyanweshi'.

hostels and boarding houses are exercising a monopoly in running their businesses. The scene is even more depressing at old age homes. Profitable ventures are being undertaken by taking advantage of the lack of security in the lives of the resident individuals. There should be an end to such hypocrisy in the name of social work. To shed light on a minor portion of this major issue, conversations were initiated with a couple of prominent individuals.

Bela-di, a boarder at the Golpark Working Girls' Hostel, said,

> In 1954, under the leadership of Sakuntala Sinha, a meeting was organised in the hall of the Muslim Institute with women from various private hostels. This meeting was chaired by Radharani Devi. The chief guest at this event was Vivekananda Mukhopadhyay, the editor of *Jugantar* at that time. The main topic of discussion was the living arrangements of working women. In this regard, the contribution and support of Debjyoti Barman, the editor of *Jugobani* magazine, was invaluable. The topic was dealt with great seriousness by various newspapers and magazines through published editorials.

The Superintendent of the C.I.T. Hostel on Christopher Road, Suprava Ghosh said,

> On 1 September 1957, the first C.I.T. Hostel was established at Christopher Road under Bidhan Roy's initiative. The Golpark Working Girls' Hostel was established in 1959. Initially, the hostel's operations were managed by a private organisation called Sarada Sangha. The C.I.T. Hostel at Bagbaazar was established in 1962. The then Superintendent of Golpark Hostel, Hashi Chakraborty, was quite strict in ensuring discipline. The names of Mira Dasgupta, Ashoka Gupta, Brahmakumari Debi, Renuka Roy, Ramla Sinha are especially noteworthy in the establishment of these hostels.

The Nari Nirjatan Pratirodh Mancha (the Forum for the Prevention of Violence on Women) and Maitrayee Chattopadhyay opined,

> The number of ladies hostels at present are not enough. The disorder at the private hostels is beyond description. We need more government hostels. At present, there are around 23 women's hostels in Kolkata. More thought should be put behind the lodging of retired single women. Apart from this, the lack of shelter for widows with children or women separated from their husbands is highly evident. Accommodation should be arranged through government initiatives by providing loans in easy instalments to working women.

The Health Secretary Lina Chakraborty said,

> It is not possible for the government to worry about every matter all the time. It is also not right to expect that the government will get everything done. Moreover, there are separate philanthropic organisations who take such matters into consideration. Even if the government takes initiative in this regard, the boarders will have to come forward themselves. The number of old age homes is not enough as per demand. Private organisations are also not a feasible option in the long run. I know that social service organisations are not fully capable of providing service to society. We need hostels, old age homes, but who will do it? The government has many responsibilities. Further, there is a lack of awareness among the masses. For me, the importance of a hospital is much more than a hostel. But, if the government builds hostels, the boarders will have to bear some of the cost so that the government's expenses are balanced.

According to this country's societal structure, women are but temporary residents of their families. This is also reflected in their own mindset. When such rootless individuals are not able to find a home in some other family, the societal quicksand does not leave them with space to stand. They are perforce made to choose between the path of suicide or other unhealthy means. Today's call is for shelter. Street children have led processions demanding shelter. There is an urgent need for these temporary residents to unite. The public should point out the wrongdoings of those social service organisations which have been using dishonest means in the name of social work. We will march forward holding the hands of those who need a tiny roof over their heads in order to shelter them from the open blue skies, the harsh sunlight, and the constant blow of torrential rains.

Home for Homeless * Home Away From Home

3
Hostel Samachar

First published in Neer Ritupatra, *3rd Issue, 1997.*

In recent times, the topic of ladies' hostels serves as an appetiser for filling up the pages of newspapers and magazines—whatever be its nutritional value! The effect is amplified if the cover page flaunts pictures of a couple of women, with a title in golden letters like 'A Dream World: Ladies' Hostels', and so on. To this add the opinions of a few renowned authors, ministers, or bureaucrats, and it sells like hotcakes!

The exact reason why these magazines are selecting the topic of ladies' hostels is not easy to comprehend, but some of these writings are definitely serving a pornographic intent. This is exactly how uninformed cinematographers portray these ladies' hostels—by depicting girls sitting around, playing cards with cigarettes in their hands, or by focusing on liquor bottles rolling on the ground with a semi-clad individual lying nearby. Thanks to media houses, this is what ordinary folks believe hostels for women are all about. In recent times, new fodder is being added to this. For instance, journalists nowadays are apparently equipped with knowledge of the artificial tools used by boarders to satiate their physical urges. It seems as if the boarders are all aliens! Legal action should be taken against reporters like these.

We expect the media to highlight the housing issues of working women and students, and suggest solutions. Instead, some media outlets aim to create a market or promote a journalist's distorted imagination—offering no real insights into hostel-related issues while reinforcing public misconceptions.

These hostel boarders mostly come from middle-class families. At least, I can say from my own experience that the boarders of B.K.B., Giribala, Mitali Boarding, Aabash, Prabashika, Sukanya, Goabagan Hostel, Nari Seva Sangha, the Bagbazar and Padmapukur C.I.T. Hostels, and Golpark Working Girls' Hostel come from middle-class and lower-class families. The precedents and perceptions created about these hostel boarders reflect the same stigmas associated with middle-class women in general. In this context, the distorted perception that hostel boarders partake in morally questionable behaviour inevitably extends to middle-class women as a whole.

The curiosity for the unknown is eternal. And if women are the inhabitants of that unknown world, that's the ultimate desire! How can journalists resist that curiosity? They even end up writing imaginary features on the topic. Moreover, nobody is really bothered about judging the facts of such stories. Therefore, whatever is presented is taken as the final truth. It doesn't seem likely that any reporter has written anything on the creative aspects of these hostel boarders till date. Additionally, nobody has even given a thought to the problems that exist at these hostels and their likely solutions.

After an agitation led by the girls at Sukanya, the honourable Housing Minister issued his statement via the media: 'It is a shame, I admit. But when it is a question of women, and outstation women at that, we certainly have to be more careful and more sympathetic. I have already asked for a report in this regard, and we have plans for improving living conditions in hostels.' (*The Statesman*, 31 August 1996).

However, even though it has been two or three months since the women from Golpark Hostel have expressed a desire to sit with the Minister in order to discuss the problems they face, the Minister has not been able to give them time. He has expressed his desire to think deeply on the existing problems at government and private hostels.

Swayambhara, an extremely popular name, is a housing facility in Salt Lake especially catering to women. It was inaugurated with great pomp and show. A huge group of women were ferried there on buses from their respective offices for the event. It is, however, slightly debatable if Swayambhara can actually be referred to as a hostel. According to its rules, students and trainees cannot avail the services of the place for more than a week, while employed women can stay up to a month. The daily bed charges at the dormitory for students and trainees is Rs 15, and Rs 25 for the employed. The other areas are lying vacant. Only ten to fifteen people can be found in the dormitory, all of whom have to go to nearby hotels for food. The monthly charge of just one bed is Rs 750. Isn't it more appropriate to refer to the premises as an upper-class resthouse! Nevertheless, our minister has assured us that he is thinking about both government as well as private hostels. Only he knows what he has been thinking! The funny thing is that one cannot arrange a meeting with the Super (superintendent) at Swayambhara. On weekdays, the Super sits from 11 am to 4 pm and does not meet people unless on a topic that is appealing to them. The topic of discussion has to be duly informed to the guard in advance by entering certain details in the register kept for that purpose.

A government hostel with single rooms has been established in Sahapur. Its monthly rent is Rs 500, which is at least Rs 150 more than what a Grade-III job pays as rent for a Type-II Quarter (Rs 250 + Rs 58 + electricity charges). Even after this, should we gloat about the fact that the government is seriously thinking about us or hostel boarders and outstation women?

One cannot begin to describe the inhumanity of these private hostels. Four individuals are forced to somehow live on four big benches or tiny versions of beds in a 10x12 foot room. Despite the unhealthy environment and water shortage, the outstation girls have no other option but to adjust. The condition of the watery dals and the vegetable 'peel' curry available at these hostels is a well-known fact. On top of that, the cooked ration rice that is served is rich in cockroach eggs, wheat, paddy, and rice grains—one has to simply pick out whatever looks appetising to them. It doesn't seem like there is a government inspection system in place to assess these businesses.

Any person who can start a women's welfare organisation and somehow manage the registration, can easily run this business. This work does not even require any sales tax, and there is no audit.

Keeping in mind these factors, the following demands are being made to the government:
1. More new hostels should be built that offer beds at the same rate as the older government hostels.
2. Workers should be employed to inspect the private hostels.
3. Every month, on a stipulated date and venue, a government representative will meet the boarders to discuss the various issues they face.
4. The food quality at private hostels will need to be improved, failing which the administration will have to leave the responsibility to the women boarders.
5. The bed count per room will have to be decreased at private hostels in order to create a healthy environment with an increased water supply. In this regard, the

government should immediately create pressure on private hostels.
6. The government will have to take charge of shifting older boarders to an old-age home or facilitate their stay in their original hostels.
7. The superintendent at every private and government hostel will have to stay at the hostel regularly, facilitate a specific meeting time, and will have to necessarily stay the night in the hostel.
8. Every hostel should set up public telephone booths for easy communication between all the hostels.
9. The return time for every hostel will need to be at least 10 pm.
10. Every hostel will have to set up a specific room for visitors.
11. Arrangements have to be made so that female boarders who are shift workers can stay in all of the hostels. To complain against any hostel that refuses her a bed, a hostel-refusal centre will have to be built.
12. Different hospitals will have reserved seats for hostel boarders.

4
Women's Development and Guruchand

First published in Chaturtha Duniya's *special memorial issue for Guruchand Thakur's birth sesquicentenary year in December 1997.*

The all-India revolution that kicked off in the nineteenth century was mainly based in cities. The effect of this city-bred, civilised people's revolutionary movement was not able to penetrate into the remote villages of Bengal. The little that reached, made its way only in the beginning of the twentieth century. A common practice in this country has been to keep a certain class of people deprived of all kinds of means and opportunities. It happens even today, especially in the case of education. Such class-based discrimination is not just typical to India but has been noticed worldwide, both in the past and the present. Although it has slightly changed its tone among well-educated society, the phenomenon is far from being eradicated. One hundred and fifty years after the birth of Guruchand Thakur, who showed the way forward to Dalits, some more Dalits have come together to evaluate him. Surprisingly, nowhere in the pages of so-called 'liberal' (!) Bengali literature, can one find a mention of Guruchand Thakur. Barring a couple of exceptions, not a single book or journal is interested in sparing an iota of space for Guruchand even today. 'The Christian missionaries were the first to attempt at introducing female education in Bangladesh. In 1891, an association by the name of Calcutta Female Juvenile Society was established in order to cater to the education of the young girls of this country' (*Bangaldesh-er Itihaas*).

It is unfortunate that one who would guide Dalits was yet to be born. Guruchand was born around the middle of the nineteenth century. In 1908, almost a century after Kolkata began championing the cause of women's education, an educational institute for Dalits (a high school) was set up through Guruchand's own efforts. The establishment of an educational institute, the propagation of female education, the advocacy of widow remarriage and the amendment of the 1911 Census Report are some of Guruchand Thakur's notable contributions.

The facts available on widow remarriage are as follows:

In the eighteenth century, Maharaja Rajballav tried to reintroduce the practice of widow-remarriage. However, the attempt proved futile because of the opposition of Krishnachandra, the Maharaja of Krishnanagar. Krishnachandra's descendent Sreeshdhar tried to marry off widows. Nilkamal Bandyopadhyay from Kolkata's Bahubajar area and many others also tried the same but failed. Shyamacharan Das, a resident of Pataldanga, tried to get his widowed daughter remarried. In 1845, the British India Society held discussions with the Dharma Sabha and the Tattvabodhini Sabha regarding the issue of widow remarriage. It was around this time that [Ishwarchandra] Vidyasagar joined the cause. In 1854, he published an essay with the *Tattvabodhini* journal in support. On 17 November 1855, when the draft of the law on widow remarriage was produced at the Byabosthapona Sabha, the whole of India saw massive movements both in its favour and against. Massive opposition also followed. After a lot of movements and debates, the Widow Remarriage Act was finally passed on 26 July 1856 (*Bangladesh-er Itihaas*).

In 1901, widow remarriage was facilitated among Dalits because of prompt action taken by Guruchand Thakur. In this regard, the available information attests that the Namashudras were referred to as 'Chandala' in the 1901 Census Report. Guruchand consulted the Australian missionary C. S. Mead about this and promised his support for widow remarriage in exchange for amendments in the Census Report. Among the people who assisted Guruchand Thakur in this matter, the names of Bidhu Chowdhury, Debichand Gosai and Gopal Sadhu need special mention. Interestingly, as noted by Mahananda Haldar in his *Sri Sri Guruchand Charit*, after the Census Report was amended, Guruchand Thakur reportedly ceased his advocacy for widow remarriage. However, this claim is debatable. Whatever be the case, Mahananda Haldar has also mentioned that Guruchand Thakur was more interested in banning the practice of child marriage than advocating for widow remarriage.

Guruchand's efforts at female education remain unmatched. Boats would be sent across the marshland to fetch female students. Apart from female education, he was also involved in the establishment of an English school for young boys. His pioneering work with regard to the Dalit education movement is the reason why people from rural areas became literates. This debt alone makes it necessary to evaluate Guruchand's *modus operandi* and character in the present age. This visionary's messages are applicable in the post-modern period too. It is very important for today's decaying and valueless society. When the polygamy practiced by higher-caste men was about to shatter the dignity of Hindu women, Guruchand gave the call for *Ek nari brahmachari* ('One woman, one bachelor').

He has also said,

> *Nij naari bhinnyo onyo naaritey gomon.*
> *Mahapaap byabhichari sei ekjon.* (*Guruchand Charit*)
>
> (Those who chase other women over their own
> As sinful adulterers are they known.)

Guruchand's father, Harichand has said,

> *Por poti por sati sporsho na koribe.*
> *Na daak horike, hori tomake dakibe.* (*Guruchand Charit*)
>
> (His spouse or hers is theirs alone,
> To practice this is to be God's very own.)

That a woman's beauty lies not in her coyness but her courage—the feminist slogan of today's progressive society—was preached by Guruchand a century ago. People of all classes should know about this person, who, despite not being educated in the modern educational style, was capable of such modern thoughts. To quote him:

> *Lojja bote naari pokkhe ekti bhusan,*
> *Onorthok lojja kintu nindar kaaron.*
> *Bir-mata hote hole hou biraangana;*
> *Byaghro singho dekhe jeno hridoy tolena.*
> *Sotityo tejete ghera jaar deho mon;*
> *Kamuk poshure bhoy kore naa kokhon.*
> *Jononi sajiya sobe koro subhodrishti,*
> *Tomaare dekhiya bishye hok shaanti bristi.*
>
> (Modesty is truly a woman's grace,
> Yet false shame brings but disgrace.
> A hero's mother must be herself bold,
> With a heart that tigers and lions can't hold.
> Whose soul shines bright with virtue's light,
> Fears no beast of lustful might.

Gaze upon the world so wise,
Let peace like rain from you arise.)

References

Haldar, Mahananda. *Sri Sri Guruchand Charit.*

Majumdar, Ramesh Chandra. *Bangladesh-er Itihaas*, 3rd volume.

5
Hyanchra Pujo in the East Bengal Tradition and a Few Wedding Songs

First published in Neer Rituaptra, *4th Issue, 1999.*

Nature worship has been a part of human civilisation since ancient times. The practice is very much alive even in the contemporary age. Observing different kinds of brata (religious fasts or observances) in different seasons has been a common practice among unmarried young women from Bengal. Some of these rituals are practised even today. These include Neel Shasthi, Ashok Shasthi, Mangal Shasthi, Ganga pujo, and Surya pujo, to name a few. Hyanchra pujo also falls under this category. It used to be practised by girls from East Bengal. I am not aware if it is still practised in East Bengal.

Unmarried girls perform the rituals for the entire month of Poush (the ninth month of the Bengali calendar) to gain a good husband. The goddess worshipped is formless. This form of worship is mainly directed at nature. A branch from the Kul tree (*Ziziphus mauritiana*) is planted in the soil and wild flowers are offered to appease the goddess. The pujo is conducted both in the mornings and the evenings. The songs that are sung are composed by the women themselves. Those who are illiterate and unable to shake off the traditions of the past, whose biggest desire is to find a handsome husband, take it upon themselves to please the Hyanchra Thairon, or goddess, to find themselves a suitable husband. These songs have existed since the times when opposing thoughts—such as finding a suitable groom is not the only destiny for women—had not yet taken root; these songs, learned from ancestors, have been passed down for a long time.

The lyrics of the songs, which have been passed down since time immemorial, are as follows:

Hyanchra Thairon lo tor
Fyaachra chul
Taite baindhye debo
Lohagoraar phul
Lohagoraar phul na
Bennar maati
Amager baap-bhai surjo shonar kaathi.

(The worshippers are telling the Hyanchra goddess that they will adorn her loose hair with wild flowers. The song ends with the hope that the precious male members of the family are blessed by her.)

Kumror phulir baashonatey
Hyanchra Thairon naachtiche
Ki bol Thairon amaare
Oi phul dey pujo debo tomaare, tomaare.

(The Hyanchra goddess' heart dances at the sight of the pumpkin blossoms, so the worshippers tell her that they will offer her the same flowers.)

Kumror phulir ponchodaal
Daal milaabo kotokaal
O malini shon na
Phul keno tol na.

(The branches of the pumpkin blossoms are heavy, the worshippers ask a girl/malini why she doesn't pluck these flowers.)

These songs used to be sung during the time of the morning puja.

The song sung in the evening is as follows:

> Saajh laaglo saaje bhai
> Sandhye gelo boiye
> Teli baari jaaiye amay tel aaine de,
> Kumor baari jaaiye amay muchi aaine de,
> Dokaane jaaiye amay chini aaine de.

(As evening is about to descend, the singer asks the listener to get her oil from the person who sells oil, a small clay pot from the potter's house, and sugar from the shop.)

If the goddess was satisfied after a month-long observation of the vows, a wedding was inevitable. The wedding songs were mainly folk songs composed by the women of the house. However, the influence of the epics on these songs is particularly noticeable. Many people are of the opinion that epics are also part of folklore, while others say that folklore has not been able to avoid the influence of the epics. Without going into this debate, given below are the few wedding songs I have been able to collect.

Sung while crushing turmeric for the wedding:

> Dhekite gaagor baaje, kuloy roton jwaale
> Kon kon aaiye kote Raam-er holud
> Ki raam re.
> Ek aaiye ache jaagar bou
> Tare ano daroga bhulaaiye
> Choukidaar dekhaaiye.
> Chit kapor urani gaay
> Jangal baaiye aaiye jaay
> Ei na aaiye jabe karo baari
> Ki raam re.
> (Graam-er naam) graame ekkhan ghor, (kono naam) matobbor
> Ei na aaiye jaabe tar baari
> Dekhiya aaiyero thant (kono naam)-er laagilo daant

Ei na aaiye thekaabe ki diye
Ei na aaiye bosaabe ki diye
(Graam-er naam)-r paan joto, ta ba ami anbo koto
Ei na aaiye thekaabo ki diye
Ki raam re.

(This song talks about how the wedding preparations are undertaken by the married women of the village who crush the turmeric for the groom, as the husking pedal roars and the lamp shines on the bamboo tray.)

Songs sung during the wedding:

Uthone boroner kulo, aaro kushi piri
Re raam tore ke sajaalo
Maa dhon to more sajaalo diye
Puror holud re, Raam tore ke sajaalo
Baba toh more sajaalo diye
Taantir saree, re Raam tore ke sajaalo
Dada toh more sajaalo diye boner maalaa
Re Raam tore ke sajaalo
Boudi to more sajaalo diye
Chutki chondone, re Ram tore ke sajaalo.

(This song talks about how the family members gift the bride with various adornments to get her ready for the wedding: a taant saree, a necklace, and sandalwood. But who helps the groom dress up?)

Juthi phule aatni, juthi phuler chutney
Champaai phul ghirilo bagichaa
raam re.
Maa dhon je bole re, Harishchandra rajaare
Tumi biye na korba, shey kaamon shundori
raam re.
Obuddhiro maa dhon re, buddhi nai tor dhore
Haare biyer ratein keba noyon mele
raam re.
Nijo deshe anibo, chanda moshaari tangaabo
Haare aena dhore dekhbo balir mukh.

(This song reflects the themes of early marriage and the transition of a young bride—bali or balika—into married life. The floral imagery may symbolise the celebratory mood of the wedding or metaphorically hint at the innocence of the child bride. It ends with the groom's anticipation of bringing her to his home and admiring her face in the mirror.)

There are many such songs and rhymes that lie scattered in every nook and corner of the green fields of rural Bengal. A spiritual pull urges me to grab onto a fraction of these, just like one would pick up tiny pebbles from the seashore. I know that my mothers and aunts had actively observed these vows and sung these songs. If I lose this tradition along with them, I will uproot my own culture and get absorbed in the jungle of weeds that have been growing in the name of culture. This is just a glance back into the past. Since I can no longer sit in the forest and offer these songs passed down by my ancestors to Hyanchra Thairon, I may as well try and hold onto them.

6
The Societal Position of Namashudra Women

---•◦●◦•---

First published in Chaturtha Duniya's *special issue on 'Dalit Women and their Security', January 2005. This essay was also presented at the Namashudra Mahasammelan in 2005, held at the Vivekananda Yuba Bharati Krirangan.*

A large section of underprivileged people around the world comprises of indigenous peoples. Among them, women remain doubly underprivileged despite being the initiators of agricultural work—civilisation's first discovery. This statement can be backed by strong evidence. In fact, one can also find a number of fables in this regard. According to one such fable acquired by Robert Briffault from among the Cherokee tribe, it was a woman who first discovered food grains in the forest. Before her death, the girl instructed that her body be dragged across the land. Wherever her body touched the soil, an abundance of crops sprouted.

Another source of evidence could be the present condition of the deprived classes. At most places, even today, agricultural work is carried out by women. One can also look for evidence in religious observances and vows. It is a common practice, not just in India, but the world over. Its origin can be traced back to ancient times. A prominent part of agricultural work in the primitive era was to observe such vows for the betterment of crops.

However, after the discovery of tools, agricultural work began shifting to the masculine domain. The matriarchal system of the ancient past also followed suit owing to the shift in inheritance practices. Ancient Rome, China, Tibet, and Africa were known for their matriarchal systems. It can still be observed among the Khasiyas.

In the southern part of China lived the Sumu people. Their queen was vested with great powers. The same was true for the Nuye-Kun people. For them, the queen's daughter would inherit her mother's throne. Marcel Granet claims that ancient China had matriarchal communities. People from China apparently named the northern part of Tibet as Nu-Gua, or 'the region of women'.

Even among Africa's deprived groups like the Agona, Lutka, Yubemra, et cetera, there is no concept of a king. All of them are ruled by a queen. The practice of marriage between siblings in ancient Egypt was also mainly a way of retaining female inheritance within the family. However, gradual cracks started appearing within matriarchal communities.

Within India, the Khasiyas have managed to hold on to the matriarchal system. For them, however, the nephew inherits the property instead of the son. This is similar to the Roman practice where the son-in-law inherits his wife's father's property instead of the son.

Ancient Indian civilisations were agriculture-based, while animal rearing was the mainstay during the Vedic age. From this it can be claimed that the ancient Indian civilisation, that is the Indus Valley Civilisation, was matriarchal whereas the Vedic Aryan society was patriarchal.

It was after the Aryan and Muslim invasions that women were pushed indoors and their freedom seized. From what can be gleaned about women as per the Vedic Brahmana texts of that age, it seems that the greatest freedom was enjoyed by prostitutes. I won't get into an extensive discussion regarding this.

A lot of information can be derived about the shudras and the Chandalas from the ancient Vedas and Charyagiti.[1] However, our topic of discussion here is the societal conditions of Namashudra women. The first usage of the name Namashudra can be traced back to the early-twentieth century, specifically to the Census Report of 1911, when the term Chandala was replaced with Namashudra. Guruchand Thakur's (1846) active intervention in this regard is particularly noteworthy. With the help of an Australia-based missionary, Dr C. S. Mead, Guruchand Thakur managed to accomplish the task of substituting Chandala with Namashudra in exchange for advocating widow remarriage. This information is available in *Sri Sri Guruchand Charit*. One wonders what would have been the issue in retaining the original name of Chandala or Chanral, as the change in terminology did not bring about any change in their state. *Sri Sri Guruchand Charit* further posits that following this, Guruchand Thakur revoked his support for widow remarriage. It is difficult to say whether this was Guruchand's own doing or merely a statement made by the book's composer, Mahananda Haldar. What poses food for serious thought is this tactical use of widows for the purpose of changing names. It seems today that perhaps retaining the term Chandala would have helped in maintaining greater kinship ties with the Haris, Doms, Muchis, and Myathors.

Annada Shankar Ray, who is known within Bengali literature and culture for his liberal mindset, exposed his attitude towards the Namashudras in the 1401 Bengali New Year edition of *Anandabazaar Patrika* by noting, 'The Namashudras are openly rebellious and aggressive

---

[1] The earliest extant Bengali poems dating back as far as the ninth century.

in nature. When a certain person went seeking their help during the riots, in return he was asked if he would consider giving them his daughter's hand in marriage'. In this matter, it must be kept in mind that these very same people who came to the Namashudras for help during riots would not even make contact with their shadows in those times.

Hemanga Biswas (an eminent Bengali folk singer), in a frank confession mentions, 'My Sonabhai, a devout Ramkrishna follower, would beat up the Namashudras for not carrying his palanquin'. At another place, we find:

> In our locality, the Namashudra subjects who were farmers, were forced to take up the job as palanquin-bearers. They collectively protested against it and refused the role. A meeting was called about 4–5 miles from my place, for this purpose. I do not remember the name of the village. Two Namashudra leaders attended the meeting from Habiganj. One of them was my batchmate—Jagadish. His presence made my job easier. Nobody else from outside the community had been invited and they were scared I would report the proceedings of the meeting to my father. That I would stand in their support was something beyond their imagination. On Jagadish's suggestion, I stood up to speak. They spoke about caste rights, injustice and oppression. I suggested expanding it to include class struggle by joining the united movement of the porters from the nearby tea garden. In this regard, the Muslim farmers were an impediment to the cause as for their weddings too, it was the Namashudras themselves who would carry their daughters in a small palanquin (we called it 'Sawari').
>
> Resultantly, the class approach did not work in this case. I realised for the first time how matters of caste can complicate class struggle.

Biswas committed the same mistake as our other leaders who try to hide caste issues behind class, instead of eradicating the former which lies at the core of our nation.

Let me first talk about those unlettered daughters of the soil who were their own teachers. These women spent a major portion of their lives giving birth. They performed rituals praying for the goodwill of their home, husband, children, and crops. Their creativity was apparent through the way they spread out dung fuel to dry, drew decorative design patterns, constructed houses, fried puffed rice, ground flattened rice, pounded turmeric, stitched quilts, wove mattresses, recited shlokas and sang at various festivals. In a culture where the festivities exceed the number of months, some of the rituals performed by the Namashudra women were:

Kulo Namaano (Putting Down a Winnowing-Tray)

In the blazing months of summer when the heat caused the ground to crack, the girls would put a winnowing-tray on their heads and pray to the clouds for relief from the drought-like condition. Such rituals for a better harvest are a common practice among indigenous people around the world. On the tray some grains and auspicious durba (bermuda) grass, a mango sheaf, betel leaf, nuts and a small pot would be neatly arranged. Moving from house to house, these women would sing a song requesting the clouds to send rains to save them from starvation and loss of animals because of drought. The song voices a heartfelt plea to the queen of the rains, describing the land as scorched by summer heat and the fields yearning for relief. It calls upon the rain to pour down and revive the earth with life and abundance.

> *Olo myagaraani shaak dhuye fela paani*
> *Shaake boro gondho, ebaar bhor khondo*
> *Ekkhaan bhuiti charkhan kona*
> *Dhan buniche kaale shona*
> *Shona lo langol goru rode pure jaay*
> *Bristire tui jhaapaay pore aay.*

The women carrying the kulo or winnowing tray on their heads, would go and stand under the corner of the roof, made of either straw or tin. The patriarch of the house or the head of the house would pour a little water at the edge of the roof—around the corner. The water would trickle down the tin roof or seep out through the pores of the straw, falling on the winnowing tray on the women's heads and they would get drenched—symbolising/manifesting rain.

Shubhochandi Pujo (The Worship of Shubhochandi)

Worshipping Shubhochandi to seek blessings for one's husband and children is a common practice in villages among Namashudras even today. This is also a kind of nature worship. This ritual is performed by using the branch of a Kul (jujube) tree as a symbol. The elements used for this ritual include betel leaves and nuts, haritaki, vermilion and oil. Women take on priestly duties and even narrate the origin story associated with Shubhochandi. Here too, the masculine principle takes over unconsciously. Keeping in mind Shubhochandi's myth, a banana is kept hidden under a wicker basket like the swan in Shubhochandi's story. At the climax of the story, this banana—standing in for the swan—is brought out and thrown away. It is then picked up by children to be eaten. These children very evidently have to be sons, not daughters. I recall an old woman named Sabitri Bakshi narrating the story in my childhood.

Hyanchra Pujo (Hyanchra Religious Ceremony)

For a farmer's family in poverty-stricken villages, the month of Poush is the month of festivals. Around this time, girls would perform the Hyanchra pujo and the boys would sing Huloi songs at night. Hyanchra pujo, like the others, is a kind of nature worship. Using wildflowers for the rituals, the girls would pray for a good husband. Craftily weaving words with great expertise, an unlettered woman by the name of Sabitri Bakshi would create the perfect ambience with Huloi songs. These songs would be composed by blending the singer's own life story with tales of characters from popular folktales, ballads and epics.

Besides these, the year-round festivities reach their finale with Poush Sankranti, Go-Fagun, Osthok, Gajon, and Charak.

Throughout the year, one can find these women neatly plastering their houses and their adjoining courtyards with cowdung mud. Their craftsmanship is also evident on the walls of the altar where the tulsi plant is enshrined in every house. They also give a variety of names to the dung fuel according to the way it is produced—like ghunte (flattened, round, or disc-shaped cakes, made by hand-pressing cow dung and mixing it with straw, then left to dry in the sun; commonly used as a fuel for cooking, especially in traditional clay stoves); b're (cow dung spread/smeared onto sticks for drying which look like kababs); and ghosi (smaller pieces and of irregular shape), et cetera.

The husking pedal, with its different parts like katla, churun, note, and so on is commonly used in villages to separate rice from the raw paddy grains. The women who are involved in the hard labour of milling rice to produce food, have a habit of singing songs during the process as a mechanism to cope with the exhaustion of the task.

Before the onset of each festival, puffed rice and flattened rice is made for the entire village to snack on. The equipment on which these jobs are accomplished also have a variety of names like khola, balyen, jhanjhor, chabna, bauli, and so on.

We get a broad picture of the societal position of Namashudras in a poetic composition by the poet Jasim Uddin. The truth exposed in the composition helps spread awareness even today. The instance of the nayeb's torture[2]

---

[2] Nayeb refers to the steward or manager of a zamindar's estate in colonial Bengal and other parts of India. Tasked with overseeing the day-to-day administration, the nayeb's responsibilities included collecting rent, managing agricultural operations,

is not just exclusive to *Sojan Badiyar Ghat* but can also be found in *Sri Sri Harililamrito*. Apart from that, Jasim Uddin's *Nakshi Kanthar Math* is an exemplary narrative about how village girls channel their sufferings through art. Their embroidery style has a diverse range of terms associated with it like swadeshi, chyalar jo, kanchir dhar, et cetera.

Different names are used for the ways the wicker mats or mattresses are woven. These include aro chyala, soja chyala, et cetera. The sweetmeats prepared during festivals too are known by different names at different places. The Jessore-Khulna region used to have kachi khocha or pitha, bhijano pithe, patishapta, puli pithe, chusi pithe, rosher jau and payesh, which can be found even today.

The light of progress gradually penetrated into this dark rural life and some girls were able to transgress, albeit in small numbers.

In 1880, Guruchand Thakur helped establish the first English-medium school for Namashudra boys in Orakandi. Before that, the boys used to study in a pathshala at Thakur's house itself. Here it must be mentioned that almost sixty-one years before this, in 1819, the Calcutta Female Juvenile Society—the first institution to impart education to women—had been set up by Christian missionaries. Guruchand Thakur established the Shanti Satyabhama M. E. Balika Vidyalaya for women's education.

Sushma Maitra Sarkar writes, 'Orakandi already had a women's organisation, of which I was the secretary.' The names of some of the women associated with the organisation from those times, as mentioned by her, include

---

and mediating disputes on behalf of the zamindar. Acting as an intermediary between the landowner and the peasants, the nayeb was crucial in maintaining the functioning of the estate, ensuring that the zamindar's interests were protected while overseeing the welfare of the tenants. It is common knowledge that these nayebs used to torture the peasants, even Thakurs such as Guruchand and Harichand Thakur's family.

Shefali Biswas, Santoskumari Talukdar, Bina Samaddar, and Dr Swarnalata Hajra. Noteworthy mentions from among other literate women are Binapani Thakur (Boro Maa), Manjulika Mallick, Hemprova Samaddar (associated with the Barisal Namashudra Samiti), and Rabiprabha Sarkar. Not much information can be found about Namashudra women after 1946, that is following the Partition of the nation.

In 1975-76, Bijoykrishna Thakur's son, Santosh Thakur, established the first Mahila Matua Sangha at Krishnachandra Thakur's house in Bagula. The women from this association would meet at each other's house in a group every Wednesday for Harisabha and read aloud from *Harililamrito*. Along with it, Santosh Thakur would advise women about ways in which they could move forward. They would play the gong and the jai-donka (a kind of drum) themselves and present Matua music. Before this, women were forbidden from playing the jai-donka and as a result no one would play it openly. Among these women, one was of brahmin origin while the others were all Namashudras. They were Nibharani (the brahmin), Subhadra Thakur, Usharani Biswas, Haridashi Sikdar, Koushalya Adhikari, Renuka Thakur, Gita Mandal, Sabitri Bakshi, Subhashini Biswas, Prabhabati Thakur and Bela Thakur. Three of them were students, the rest were housewives.

The economic and social security of a large section of Namashudra women, all of them Partition victims, is in danger. A section of them work as domestic workers in the suburbs. Many of them were abandoned by their husbands. Another section of these women are vegetable vendors. It is not difficult to identify them as most of them wear the typical coconut-bead necklaces—a well-known Matua symbol. Besides, the domestic workers who travel along the Bangaon line keep humming songs by Bijoy Sarkar, Aswini Gosai, et cetera. Regular commuters on this line would have experienced this.

It is important to mention those whose social security is in jeopardy today. This began with the introduction of dowry. Not just female infanticide, but a large number of girls are also being trafficked outside Bengal by touts. Some of them end up in brothels in other states, while others find themselves as the second wife of men from foreign lands who already have wives and children. The family members of these women are equally a part of these rackets. Thanks to television, people are aware of this issue nowadays.

The number of women who entered the literary domain is also insignificant in number. I have tried to put together a list of writers and their works:

1. Sushma Maitra Sarkar
   Mon Mukure (essay collection, 1993)
   Ek Ekke Ek (a collection of stories)
2. Kiranmoyi Talukdar
   Biswamohamondole Matuadhormo (a work of research, 1987)
   Jannayak Mukundobihari Mallick: Jibon o Sadhona (1988)
   Kabirmanishi (2001)
3. Bina Roy Sarkar
   Daak Diye Jai (an anthology of stories, poems and essays)
4. Shipra Biswas
   Anneshon (a work of research)
5. Manju Bala
   Churno Samudrer Dheu (a book of verse)
   Uttaran (play)
   Chorabali (a collection of stories)
   Oswarohir Opekkhay (a book of verse)
6. Jharna Haldar
   Pratikkhay Bishonno Bikel (a book of verse; joint publication/Andaman)

7. Sujata Biswas
   Naraker Alo (a book of verse)
8. Kalyani Thakur
   Dhorlei Juddho Sunishchit (a book of verse, 2003)
   Oshwo Series (a book of verse, 2004)
   Je Meye Adhar Gone (a book of verse, 2000)
   Chandalinir Kobita (a book of verse, 2011)
   Krishnachandra Thakur (Keshto Sadhu) Smriti Sombhar (essays in memory of Krishnachandra Thakur edited with Manohar Mouli Biswas, 1999)
   Loksangskritik Probondho Sonkolon (volume of essays on folklore)
   Matua Dharmaprosonge (edited volume of essays on Matua religion)
9. Nilima Sarkar
   Rickshawalar Bou (novel)
   Kaljoyi Obokkhyoy
   Sudureo Tomar Chithi Ashe (a book of verse)
   Meghbristir Pakhi (a book of verse)
10. Hemprova Niyogi
    Baba Saheb Dr. B. R. Ambedkarer Nirbachit Chinta Bhabna (an edited volume)
11. Swarnamoyi Mandal
    Archana (a book of verse)
    Protidhwani (a book of verse)
    Smritilipi (a book of verse)
    Padmadighi (a book of verse)
12. Lili Haldar
    Purnagrash (a book of verse)
    Rakhaler Landscape (a book of verse)
    Nimfuler Gondho (a book of verse)
13. Suniti Poddar
    Chokher Aloy (a book of verse)
    Aaj Boro Duhshomoy (a book of verse)

Bhangagora Swapnera (a book of verse)

Nihsongo Raat Jagiye Rakhe (a book of verse)

Apart from these, women who have occasionally written for various newspapers and magazines are Shefali Sarkar, Bibha Biswas, Alaknanda Roy, Kanan Boral, Dipali Haldar, Paromita Baidya, Rabiprabha Sarkar, Sabita Bhakta, and Sujata Dhar among others.

Among the women associated with the editorial board of various little magazines and journals, the ones listed below need special mention.

Chaturtha Duniya – Kalyani Thakur Charal
Ekhon Tokhon – Manju Bala
Dour – Dipika Biswas
Neer Ritupatro – Kalyani Thakur Charal
Surja – Pushpa Bairagya (as a co-editor)
Matangini – Tapashi Sarkar
Pakhir Aakash – Basudha Biswas
Dalit Jagran – Smritikona Howladar
Sailadoho – Nilima Sarkar
Abhi – Ashalata Roy
Driptokantha – Shipra Gayen
Arunkanti – Suniti Poddar

Some names associated with Dalit music, folk music and Kobigaan[3] are Sambiti Poddar, Pipasha Biswas, Sandhya Sarkar, Manisha Biswas, Arati Thakur, Uma Majumdar, and Nilima Biswas.

In politics, the names of Ashalata Majumdar, Bibha Biswas, Gita Biswas, Rama Biswas, Kalyani Biswas, Gouri Hawladar, Anima Mandal, Sandhya Mandal, Chapala Majumdar, and Pranita Roy are especially mentionable.

Apart from this, a large group has become recently involved with the panchayat, even though they work as representatives of different political groups.

---

[3] A folk performance from Bengal with a verbal duel among poets.

In theatre, the notable names would be Namita Das, Sima Das, Ashima Das, Aparna Roy, Dipa Mallick, Miss Mary, Anima Biswas, Pubali Biswas, Kaberi Ghorami, Chandana Poddar, Supriti Roy, Archana Sarkar and Kalyani Biswas.

If one has to cite examples from those who have carved a niche for themselves as social workers and activists Kalyani Mandal's name cannot be missed. She created headlines for leading a protest in Barrackpore School to stop the Saraswati Puja celebrations. Mandal is also closely connected with the rationalist association.

Lila Biswas was a fellow worker during the flood relief campaign. Lilabati Biswas has been silently working towards the uplift of Dalits by hosting various meetings of Dalit movements at her house for a very long time. Despite being a resident of Delhi, Nirupama Biswas has been voluntarily working for the betterment of society in West Bengal. Namashudra women who have managed to acquire a higher education and are travelling abroad are our pride. Among them, the names that stand out are Dr Ashmita Mitra, Dr Monika Mishra, and Sima Das. IAS officer Ranu Biswas is also the pride of the community.

In 1996, the first All India Dalit Women's Sammelan happened in Batala, in Punjab, under the Dalit Solidarity Programme. Five women from the north-eastern part of the country participated in this conference. Three of them were Namashudras, namely Manju Bala, Sujata Sarkar and yours truly. On 12 July 1996, I was invited to chair a session at this conference. The conference saw the participation of renowned personalities from all over India. Among them were Jyoti Lanjewar (Maharashtra), Urmila Pawar (Maharashtra), Kusum Meghwal (Rajasthan), Sushila Takbhore (Madhya Pradesh), and Vimal Thorat (JNU). Apart from them, Ramdas Athawale and Achintya Biswas also attended along with their families.

At the All India Backward and Minority Communities Employees Federation (BAMCEF)'s Patna session in 2002, the other participants apart from me included Lilabati Biswas and Namita Das. Besides this, there are many others who are well established in their own chosen fields. However, I must frankly admit my ignorance about their whereabouts. Given the fact that most of these people remain isolated, the whole picture is unclear for us.

Even those who tried to project a progressive liberal mindset by citing the Marxist class struggle, were unable to transcend Indian casteism. A large section of the population which lies at the core of the class struggle, consists of people from lower castes along with women. Hence, unless more awareness is generated about the caste situation and efforts are made to change the structure of patriarchal society, just spreading awareness about class will not be enough. It will only propel us further backwards.

References

Ananda Bazaar Patrika, Pahela Baisakh 1401.

Bhattacharya, Sukumari. *Prachin Bharat: Samaj o Sahitya.*

Biswas, Hemanga. *Ujaan Gang Baiya.*

Chattopadhyay, Debiprasad. *Shey Juge Mayera Boro.*

Das, Nareshchandra. *Namashudra Sampraday o Bangladesh.*

Haldar, Mahananda. *Sri Sri Guruchand Charit.*

Ray, Nihar Ranjan. *Bangalir Itihaas (Adi Parva).*

Sarkar, Kavirasraj Tarakchandra. *Sri Sri Harililamrito.*

Sarkar, Sushma Maitra. *Mon Mukure.*

Sharma, Ramsharan. *Prachin Bharote Shudra.*

Shastri, Shibnath. *Ramtanu Lahiri o Totkalin Bongosomaj.*

Thakur, Kapilkrishna, ed. *Chaturtha Duniya* (Issue on Guruchand).

7
Matua Philosophy and Today's Politics

First published in Matua Dharma Prasango, *edited by Kalyani Thakur, 2010.*

The materialistic side of Matua philosophy has a social and political link. It is highly evident that politics has a link with religion all over the world. It is difficult to find a leader who has not used religion as a weapon in the governance of the state. For some it has been direct, for others subtle. There is no exception in the case of the Matua religion too.

Foreword

The fact that the emergence of the Matua religion served as an opposition to Hindu religion can be easily proven by putting the spotlight on Matua literature. Ramakanta Bairagi from Mukhdoba village used to perform Basudev pujo. There is a mention in *Sri Sri Harililamrito* about the attitude of contemporary brahmins who opposed this puja by the untouchables. Ramakanta would offer bhog to Basudev with the banana plant stem, banana blossom, bananas and sunned rice. One day, a brahmin happened to chance upon this. The events that followed are narrated thus:

> Ekdin graambaashi Bipra ekjon
> Basudev bhograag korilo dorshon.
> Krodh kori bole Bipra 'E kon bichaar'.
> Shudrer ki aache onnobhog odhikaar?
> Shudra hoye Basudev onno dili raadhi.
> Kothaay shunili beta emoto obidhi.
> Haay re bairaagi tor eto okalyaan.
> Shudra hoye hobi naaki brahman samaan.
> Brahman kohilo giyaa brahman shokole.
> Shuniya brahman shob krodhe uthe jwole.
> Jon dosh Bipra gelo Goswaamir baari.
> Krodhbhore Basudev loye elo kaari.
> Goswami nirmal chitte dilen chariyaa.
> Bolilo, 'Re Pranbashu! Sukhe thak giyaa'.
> Chirodin rakhiyaacho brahmoner maan.
> Jao jao Bipra ghore nahi opomaan.
> Keho bole, 'Rakho debe protistha koriye.
> Jaati geche Namashudrar pokko onno kheye.' (30–31)[1]

Ramakanta Bairagi was the guru of Jaswant, Harichand's father. There is a myth that it was his boon that led to the birth of Harichand. It is important to mention here that, even today, the person in charge of preparing the bhog prasad at various missions or religious festivals is necessarily a brahmin. In this matter, the subject of midday meal is especially relevant.

---

[1] A brahmin villager once chanced upon an untouchable serving offerings to the idol of god Basudev. This angered him as such rights were only available to the brahmins. He went and spread the news among other brahmins, and the angry bunch went to the untouchable's house to snatch back the idol. The untouchable let go of the idol, wishing that the god was happy wherever he went.

Buddha and Harichand

Let's shed some light on Buddha's idea of socialism as contained within *Sri Sri Harililamrito*.

> Neech hoye koribo je neecher uddhaar.
> Oti nimne na namile kishe avataar?
>
> Neecho jon ucche hobe Buddha toposhyay.
> Buddhadeb avataar je shomoy hoy.
> Buddher kaamonaa taha poripurno jonyo.
> Jashomanta grihe Hori hoilo obotirno.
> Buddhadeb bohudin tapashya korilo.
> Taatey Brahma pronobaadi shudretey paailo.
> Neechjon proti doya Buddhadeb kore.
> Pranabete odhikaari shudra taar pore.
> Buddhadeb tapashyate hoiya sodoy.
> 'Borong Grihu' bole probhu bor ditey chaay.
> Buddha bole, 'Bor jodi dibe mahashoy,
> Ogrobhabe koro prabhu shudrer upaay.'
>
> Prabhu bole, 'Tobo naame avataar hobo.
> Pranab trigunnaam shudrere bilbaao'.
>
> Buddha bole 'Jodi prabhu hou avataar.
> Edeshe thaakena jeno jaatir bichaar' (39–40)[2]

---

[2] Unless one lowers themselves to the level of the lowest, they cannot understand the real condition of the people from the margins and cannot truly become an avatar. When Buddha came to Earth as an avatar, lower-caste people got a chance to uplift themselves. His prayers led to the birth of Harichand in the house of Jashomata Biswas. Buddha prayed for the rights of shudras. Pleased with his prayers, when the lord wanted to grant him a boon, Buddha requested the welfare of the shudras be upheld. God accepted his request and declared his decision to be born in the human world and show the way ahead to the shudras. Buddha requested again that if God did as he said, he should make sure that caste divisions are erased forever.

The fact that the Matua religion was inspired by Buddhism has been explained in detail by Kavirasraj Tarakchandra Sarkar. This religion was conceived as an opposition to casteism, in order to escape the vicious cycle of Hinduism. This was why Harichand Thakur had taken birth.

Buddha's principles lie embedded within *Tripitaka* in this fashion:

1. A free religion is essential for a free society.
2. All religions are not acceptable.
3. Religion should have a connection with the daily, real events of life rather than god, soul, theories related to heaven or earth, or imagination.
4. A religion should never be centred on god, the redemption of the soul, or animal sacrifices.
5. It is not within scriptures but in a person's heart where true religion exists.
6. Humans and morals will most definitely have to be at the centre of a religion or else it will turn into barbaric superstitions.
7. Moral values as one's life philosophy is not enough. Since there is no god, morality will have to be the law binding one's life.
8. A religion's responsibility lies in reconstructing the world and spreading happiness all around—to explain its creation or destruction.
9. Conflict of interest is the reason behind the prevailing unhappiness in the world and the only way to eradicate it is by following the Eightfold Path.
10. The private ownership of property brings power to one class and misery to the other.

11. For the well-being of the world, one must identify the reason behind sadness and eradicate it.
12. All human beings are the same.
13. It is not birth but one's merit that is the criterion upon which an individual is evaluated.
14. One's high ideals are much more important than their lofty lineage.
15. One must never give up their friendship with everyone, even if it is their enemy.
16. Every person has the right to education. Just like food, an individual needs education to survive.
17. An education that is separated from character is dangerous.
18. Nothing is infallible, nothing is imperative for eternity; everything is subject to inquiry or examination.
19. Nothing is eternal, everything is subject to change.
20. War is unjust if not fought for justice or truth.
21. The victor has a duty towards the vanquished.

What remains of Marxian theory is a small remnant of the fire but a very important one. According to me, the remains of this theory can be traced within four topics:

1. The task of philosophy is not to explain the origin of the world, but to reconstruct the world.
2. There is a conflict of interest between each class.
3. Private ownership of property brings power to one class and misery to another through exploitation.
4. The welfare of society requires the abolition of private ownership of property in order to eradicate misery.

What is left of the essence of Marxian theory are: (a) envy; (b) dictatorship of workers.

The Matuas are mainly farmers, fishermen, sharecroppers, rickshaw-pullers, vegetable vendors, labourers, florists, domestic workers, and so on. In a sense, they are all more or less from the labouring class, that is workers or servants. Moreover, there is no need to explain that the dictatorship of these workers has not been established in this country yet and that most of them are unorganised workers. In comparison, the Matuas are more organised in terms of religiosity, thanks to the association introduced by Guruchand. Hence, instead of being subservient to a brahmanical political party's dominance, the empowerment of Dalits through their self-identification will be the key to the establishment of Matua ideals in the truest sense. A society which sells itself by sacrificing its ideals, does not go far. It brings temporary gains definitely, but for the larger population, it only brings forth misery.

The Matuas and Today's Politics

Guruchand pointed to a house north of Ghritakandi and asked a Kayasth businessman, Girish Basu, to start a school. Girishbabu was a businessman from Kolkata. He went to the village to discuss the possibility of building a school and a charity hospital with Guruchand. The explanation of how this school moved to Fukra village because of the conspiracy of the brahmins can be found in *Sri Sri Guruchand Charit*:

> Brahman Kayastha aadi borno Hindu joto
> Namashudra proti hingshaa kore je shototo
> Podotole pisto kori raakhibaare chaay
> Namoh-r unnoti hole bishe dohe kaay
> Orakandi hote dure Fukra graametey
> Brahman Kayastha baash kore eksaathe
> Hingshuk Brahmon joto bhaabe mone mon
> Uccha shikkha paay jodi Namashudra-gon

Kichutey nistaar mora nahi pabo aar
*Namashudra koribek shob odhikaar.*³

Guruchand's plan was to establish a school through Girish Basu. The scheming brahmins conspired to provide for only a health centre instead of the educational institution.

Lekhaaporaa nahi jaane boka otishoy
Sikkhito hoile era moder hobe daai
Jomi-jot nahi haatein haal nahin dhori
Era jodi hoye boshe raj kormochaari
Haatein-bhaate maaraa jaabo nahik sondeho.
Brahmohatya hobe seshe taai tumi koho?
Nitanto bhabna jodi aashe tobo mone
Ek kaaj koro jaa boli ekhone
Datobyo-chikitsagriho deho shei thaai
Taar cheye punyokormo aar kichu naai
Roge shoke more jeeb koto kosto peye
Taara shob beche thak oushudi kheye
Bidyadaan tucchyo kotha prandaan hobe,
*Punyo phole ontekale sworge chole jaabe.*⁴

Instead of letting education be an eye-opener, it was better to resuscitate them while leaving them in a dying state.

---

³ All the higher caste people are extremely jealous of the Namashudras and want to keep them under their dominance. They never want the Namos to prosper. From Orakandi to Fukra, the brahmins and the Kayasths live together. The jealous brahmin lives in constant anxiety that the Namashudras will receive education and liberate themselves, which will lead to them snatching all the power from the brahmins.

⁴ They are uneducated and quite foolish. If they receive education, they will become a burden for the upper castes as they will find white collar jobs and leave the others jobless. It will amount to the death of the brahmins or brahmohatya, which is considered a grave sin. If at all something must be done for them, it is best to establish a charity hospital which will look after their physical well-being. This will be of greater virtue than educating them, as saving life earns one a place in heaven.

The reason why this topic has been chosen is to narrate the story of the Matua community's wants and desires in the present age. Why, suddenly, after 150–200 years have the Matuas or Harichand–Guruchand resurfaced from their graves? The story has been presented by various media houses with wrong information, especially by *Bartaman* and *Anandabazaar Patrika*. It is important to know why the Matuas from India today have become newspaper fodder after sixty-two years of Independence; its political and religious context needs to be exposed in front of the public, especially the Matuas.

In the year 2003, when the Citizenship Amendment Bill began to designate post-1971 refugees as 'Illegal Migrant(s)', the Matua Mahasangha and an organisation called the Udvastu Sangram Samiti declared an indefinite hunger-strike with twenty-one members from 15–21 December 2004, when the winter session of Parliament was underway. The intention behind this was to safeguard Indian voters of thirty years from the harassment that could befall them as a result of this black law. The timing was strategically selected during the ongoing session so that before the bill—which had been unanimously ratified by all forty-two Members of Parliament from West Bengal—became law, the state could present its own bill in opposition. At that time, apart from Mamata Banerjee, there were also other leftist members in Parliament. It is very sad that at that time no Bengali representative of any political party came forward to address the crisis faced by the Bengali refugees. I am repeatedly using the word Bengali here because the refugee crisis or the crisis faced by the Bengalis was due to the Partition of Bengal. The people were not responsible for it. Useless leaders were responsible. Even today, these people's representatives continue with such trashy business. This issue stems from the ethnic crisis faced by Dalits. Since the upper-caste leaders don't even think about these refugees—all lower-caste Bengalis—as Bengalis, why sue a beggar and catch a louse? They know that these refugees are almost all Dalits. Even the newspapers did not shoulder the responsibility of making people aware of this terrible law. To stop this movement, the Matuas were advised, 'You are a religious organisation. Why would you enter politics? Instead, build a temple with the money we provide'. Not only did the political movement of the Matuas change course, Dalits who were more aware were also misled by the brahminical political parties continuing to make one joke after the other. The Matuas withdrew from the original movement, undermining the interests of the larger population.

This is similar to how the building of a school was replaced by a charity hospital, as mentioned in *Sri Sri Guruchand Charit*. The Matua Mahasangha continues to settle for small gifts instead of its real demands, and increasingly grows non-committal about representing the entire Dalit community. If today the Matua Dalits start dancing to the tunes of the brahminical politicians, not only will they go astray from the path shown by Guruchand, they will be unable to represent Dalits, especially the Namashudra community. This is in light of the fact that a small number of people holding leadership positions in the Matua Mahasangha cannot take the decision of misguiding an entire Dalit population for the sake of their own petty interests. Even Boro Maa[5] herself cannot pave the way for all the Matuas to become slaves of brahminical political parties solely for her familial gain. Because the cunning brahmins have never used Dalits for any reason other than their own interests.

Till date, no Bengali progressive, reformist politician or brahminical politician from Bengal, or even intellectuals, have come forward with the aim of attempting to amend the Citizenship Amendment Act of 2003. If this remains

---

[5] The matriarch of the Matua Mahasangha.

unresolved, the fate of a large number of Matuas and refugee Bengalis will soon head towards a disaster and the reason behind this will be those who are doing politics under the guise of the Matua Mahasangha and Boro Maa. Because if Dalits turn against the interests of those brahminical politicians or try to gain political power for themselves, then the law will start being put into force. What could be the ultimate example of treason if not this case, where these politicians are not thinking twice before labelling their large number of voters, who have been their vote bank for thirty long years, as 'Illegal Migrant(s)'?

The Matuas also need to understand why the different media houses never wrote about them all this while. Where only Thakur's pictures were being advertised at the expense of the Mahasangha prior to the Baruni Mela, suddenly newspapers began mentioning the Matuas; not for the Matuas themselves but because of Brinda Karat, Biman Bose, Ashok Ghosh, and Mamata Banerjee. Hence, instead of getting carried away by this compensatory gesture, the greater need is to delve deep and deliberate on what Guruchand has said.

These upper-caste leaders who created this crisis for the refugees, and in turn the Matuas, have become the object of hatred of leaders of other states across India by causing the Matuas to vocalise their problems with their actions, thereby providing a wake-up call for the ruling class. These people have started doling out breadcrumbs. Why have there been no roads, no educational centres, no stadiums named after Harichand–Guruchand for so long? Why have their names not found a place anywhere in history for almost two hundred years? Despite such storms being raised in the names of Harichand–Guruchand, will the education, health and economy of the people from Dalit-dominated areas improve? Will they be put behind bars for merely talking about development? If these Matuas remain satisfied with these insignificant crumbs instead of starting a fight for their self-esteem, these upper-caste leaders will be able to continue their rule for some more time.

Babasaheb has said, 'My people are asleep, hence I am awake all night as they need to be woken up.' Guruchand had done that almost one hundred and fifty years ago. It is because of him that twenty-nine Dalits became MLAs in undivided Bengal. When it became evident that Dalits were occupying powerful political positions, the call for Bengal's Partition was made, thereby obstructing the growing power of the Dalits. The high-caste leaders of those times like Nehru, Syama Prasad or even P. R. Thakur's opposition to Jogen Mandal destroyed the path of development for Dalits. Even today, if the Matuas start acting as foot soldiers for the Gandhiwadis and the Marxists, instead of bringing together the ideologies of Babasaheb and Guruchand, maybe two or three Matua Gosains[6] will benefit at the expense of the interests of numerous Dalits and refugee Matuas. The Matuas are not aliens. They are people belonging to the Dalit Bahujan society. While referring to them, Kanshiram-ji had long ago turned towards Bengal and mentioned the names of these two great men in the same ranks as Jyotirao Phule and Periyar Ramasamy. If the Matuas act as vassals of the upper-caste politicians, they will only cause harm to the larger population of the Dalit community. This is because by misleading them and keeping them pacified with small gifts, the upper-castes will keep their kingdom intact. In that case the Banerjees, the Bhattacharyas, and the Mukherjees will continue to remain in their leadership positions like old wine in new bottles. The golden boat that Guruchand had made us dream of will sink before reaching its destination because of these selfish Gosains. Therefore, the only way to increase the strength of the Bahujan

---

[6] Well-versed in theological scholarship, the Gosains are regarded as messengers to Matua disciples.

community will be by not selling out the Matua movement but including it within the Bahujan movement and taking the right steps towards the development of the entire Dalit community as a collective; by sacrificing self-interests in the favour of one's community and continuing to fight for one's self-esteem instead of joining the Gandhis, just like Guruchand. The Matua Gosains know very well that even this year many refugees have been arrested in Burdwan and Goskara in the name of this law. They have been released recently, but the law has not changed. The Matuas need to be more politically aware. This is what Thakur had wanted and hence he had said,

Aayin shobhaay jaao, ami boli, raajaa hou.

Go to the seats of justice, I say, become rulers.

Why can't a Matua person of the same mentality take the lead in rescuing these fallen people? To row their boats even today a person from the other caste is needed whose eyes are on the royal seat and on ways to resist Dalits. When Mayawati demonstrates her majority in numbers, they say 'Victory to the evil power!' We do not feel ashamed.

Progressive Bengal's strategy of exploitation is different. We repeatedly set foot in that trap. They point fingers at the underdeveloped states of Bihar and Uttar Pradesh where Dalits are in power, diverting our attention, and we eat it up. We lose sight of Amalashol, Lalgarh, Singur, Nandigram, Sundarbans. Marichjhapi's blood has dried up. That's why the refugee Matuas have forgotten the actions of that government. They give in to their temptations again: the very same people who brought back thousands of refugees only to shoot them without a thought; those who repeatedly evicted them, kept them illiterate, threw new problems their way, distracting them, blocking their way forward by creating group conflicts and thereby unleashing new strategies of exploitation. It hurts deeply when the Matuas surrender to these temptations laid out for them by these people.

The fight for self-esteem has just begun. The shudras have just awoken. As a way of blocking job prospects, privatisation has started where there will be no reservation. Meanwhile, there has been a sudden burst of providing caste certificates. Dalits will roam around with their birthmark, the caste certificates, hanging around their necks but find no jobs. In the hands of businessmen like Tata, ancestral lands will disappear in the name of development. Then the Bhattacharyas and the Banerjees will start bargaining again. From an agricultural worker, the Dalit son will become an industrial worker. We will still remark that there has been development. The dream of becoming our own masters will not be entertained. These people will remain slaves for life and serve the upper castes. They will cast their votes year after year because they will suddenly find themselves being cast as labour leaders in a classic strategic move. Will the Matuas still keep their eyes shut and ask us to cast our votes in favour of these upper-caste politicians? Arise, people, and awake! Instead of being used as mere vote banks, help Dalits dream of fighting for their own power. When things like economy, politics and education are needed, how can one act as an intermediary to increase the votes of others?

References

Ambedkar, B. R. *Buddha na Karl Marx*, translated by Samar Chandra Roy.

Haldar, Mahananda. *Sri Sri Guruchand Charit.*

Sarkar, Kavirasraj Tarakchandra. *Sri Sri Harililamrito.*

 Scan the QR code to hear Kalyani Thakur Charal and Anurima Chanda read excerpts from this chapter.

8

How Applicable is Western Feminism in a Caste-Divided Society?

First published in Chaturtha Duniya Patrika, *Number 38, edited by Amar Biswas, 2010*

Manu's devaluation of women and shudras is responsible for determining the position of women in the Hindu society. In contrast, among various tribes, the position of women is elevated, and even in the division of property women's rights are prioritised. For example, one can talk about the Khasias, the Agonnas from Africa, the Lotukas, and other ethnic groups.

The word patriarchy means ruled by men. The word can be traced back to the Latin root 'pater'. But according to feminist theorists, 'patriarchy' refers to male domination that seeks to control women in every way. Feminist theorist Sylvia Walby has written in her book *Theorizing Patriarchy* (1990), 'patriarchy is such a social and political system in which men control women, oppress them and exploit them'. Walby wants to look at patriarchy as a system.

Friedrich Engels, in his book *The Origin of the Family, Private Property and the State*, clearly notes that the day matriarchy was defeated was the day when women were defeated in the history of the world. The authority of the household passed into the hands of men, the dignity of women degraded and thus began the slavery of women.

A great difference can be observed between the terminology of feminist philosophers and the terminology of social scientists. At the root of Aristotle's philosophy is the idea that men were born to rule this earth. And that women were born to accept the slavery of men: 'The courage of man is shown in commanding, of a woman in obeying'.

Later, an example of Freud's mentality came to the surface: 'For women, anatomy is destiny.' He said that men are 'Natural Human(s)' and women are 'Deviant Human(s)'. Freud also said that women become intensely jealous of the male sex organ and that jealousy weakens women: '... a deviant human being lacking a penis, whose entire psychological structure supposedly centres around the struggle to compensate for this deficiency.' Philosophers have staunchly protested against this notion about a woman's psychology. A child does not come into this world with feminine or masculine qualities. Rather, it is society that creates a woman. As feminist thinker Simone de Beauvoir has said, 'One is not born, rather becomes a woman!'

Marx and Engels were able to show only one way to end patriarchy; 'Once private property was abolished, and women joined the labour force, patriarchy would disappear. The primary contradiction for them was not sex but between class.' However, the applicability of this principle in a multi-ethnic country like India needs to be considered.

Gail Omvedt visited different places in India and established three ideas about the origins of patriarchy:
1. The society of the Paleolithic or pre-Paleolithic age was matriarchal in nature without any gender discrimination.

2. Classless, casteless, and genderless societies existed only as long as the stateless social system existed up until the Stone Age or later. Even after the birth of the state, the influence of patriarchy did not develop. Rather, the power of women in society was predominant.
3. After the creation of the state and social classes, economic inequality began to increase in society. Armies were formed, and religious influence in society grew. Alongside this, a form of authority over women also began to rise. This authority is called patriarchy, which, in Gail Omvedt's terminology, refers to the establishment of male dominance over women's reproductive power, sexuality, and labour. Feminist theorists have differing opinions on the interpretation of patriarchy, but they envision a future where there will be no state, no class, and no concept of gender inequality. Such a society is possible because such societies existed in the past.

The proponents of the concept called bourgeois feminism, whose main goal has been to analyse women's problems in the light of gender inequality, believe that:
1. The women's liberation movement is different from the movement for socio-economic infrastructure.
2. Men are the enemies of women. It is male society that has established patriarchy. As a result of the establishment of male dominance, women have been reduced to a kind of house arrest. Men exploit women and women are the ones who are exploited. There is no such thing as class in this case.
3. There is a need to unite against patriarchy. There is no class struggle here. Women constitute a different class altogether.
4. A movement for women's liberation is a movement aimed at solving the problems faced by every woman. The movement by workers, peasants, lower-class

women, and middle-class women are not different movements.
5. This type of movement demands individual freedom for the liberation of women in this system; that is the desire to change the status of women by making legal amendments within the existing social infrastructure; that is, a couple of reforms like the right to vote, the right to property, the right to abortion, the right to divorce, so on and so forth.

In addition, the seeds of the movement that were sown among the working class with the rise of capitalism gave rise to a new thought among working-class women which was led by Clara Zetkin, Rosa Luxemburg, Alexandra Kollontai, Nadezhda Krupskaya and others. It can be said that the theory of Karl Marx and Friedrich Engels is at the root of the women's liberation movement which developed from Marxist class analysis and the reaction against the discrimination of women.

In 1848, Jyotirao Phule opened a girls' school at Bhideji's house in Pune. A second school was established in 1851. In 1851 itself, girls got the opportunity to sit for exams at the school established by Phule. This is how education started to spread among Dalit women. Jyotirao educated his wife Savitribai Phule and his cousin, Sagunabai, so they could provide education to the girls. They are the mothers of Dalit feminism.

Meanwhile in Bengal, in 1819, the Christian missionaries set up the Calcutta Female Juvenile Society, the first school for female education. In the year 1886, under the initiative of the Brahmo Samaj and Swarna Kumari Devi's leadership, the Ladies Association was established in Bengal. *Bamabodhini* magazine was published under her editorship.

The Sarada Sadan and Mukti Sadan were established in Bombay under the initiative of Pandita Ramabai. The All India Women's Organisation was formed in 1917, with

Annie Besant as its president. Margaret Cousins was their editor. The Women Council of India was formed in Bombay in 1920. In 1925, the first All India Women Council (AIWC) was established under the initiative of Margaret Cousins.

Soviet women started their own Soviet Women Anti-Fascist Committee. In Paris in 1945, an international conference was held with 850 women representatives from 181 organisations spanning forty countries worldwide. This conference saw the birth of the Women's International Democratic Federation (WIDF) which catered to women from all over the world.

The year 1975 was declared as International Women's Year. 1975–85 was declared the International Women's Decade. This declaration had a huge impact on the women's movement in India. Various women's organisations began to come into existence. A state of emergency was declared in 1975–77. The rights of individuals and organisations were curtailed because of which none of the organisations could sustain themselves during that time.

Sushma Maitra Sarkar writes in *Mon Mukure*,

> There is proof in the minutes of the Juvenile Society for the year 1821, 14 December. The report shows that in 1820, the school started with only eight students. In 1821, the numbers rose to thirty-two. Among the students were women from the Bagdi, Vaishnav, Chandala communities, and a couple of Brahmin, Kayasth and old women.

> But as the girls from the so-called aristocratic families did not come to school openly, there was an organisation called the British and Foreign School Society in London which sent Ms Mary Ann Cook to Calcutta to spread education.

She further writes,

> In the year 1945 of the English calendar, on the occasion of the arrival of Babasaheb Bhimrao Ramji Ambedkar, a grand meeting was organised under the initiative of the Scheduled Federation of the Gopalganj sub-division of Faridpur district. The event saw the participation of more than 40,000 scheduled castes. I attended this meeting as a

Secretary on behalf of the Orakandi Women's Federation with a bunch of money. This event was organised and led by Jogendranath Mandal.

The other women who attended the event with Sarkar were Santosh Kumari Talukdar, Bina Samaddar, Pritilata Haldar, Prabhati Biswas, Kamala Bagchi, Swarnalata Hajra, Sefali Biswas and others.

In terms of how women were regarded, we can see from Gautam Buddha's time to this day how Gautama Buddha accepted the invitation of a courtesan while ignoring the invitation of the king, and not only that, under his guidance women were allowed to take the pabbajja.[1] The first works by women were the *Therikatha*, composed by Buddhist women.

Next, if we turn our eyes to the Matua religion, we can see how Harichand Thakur (1812–78) had organised a protest meeting with women when his devotee Dasharatha was tortured by the Naib. We find a narration of this incident in great detail in *Sri Sri Harililamrito* written by Tarakchandra Sarkar.

Guruchand Thakur (1846–1937), son of Harichand Thakur, established the Shanti Satyabhama Girls' School in the name of his mother Shanti Devi and wife Satyabhama Devi. Here, vocational education was also provided. Guruchand Thakur brought girls from the untouchable community and started the initiative of educating them. Not only that, Guruchand Thakur encouraged devotees to perform widow remarriages under the inspiration of the Australian missionary C. S. Mead.

During the nineteenth century, when Hindus were practicing polygamy and forcing widows to commit Sati, Harichand Thakur proclaimed 'Ek Nari Brahmachari' ('One woman, one bachelor'). He also preached, 'Koribe garjostho

---

[1] The Buddhist ceremony where an ordinary person gains preliminary ordination as a novice.

dhormo loye nijonaari, grihe thaake nnyashi, banprosthi, brohmochaari' ('Sincerely observing one's familial duties with one's wife is equivalent to practicing the life of a mendicant, a Vanaprastha, or a Brahmacharya without renouncing one's domestic life').

Periyar E. V. Ramasamy (1879–1973) emphasised dismantling various social norms to increase the power of women, so that not only are women valued more but that the social system would come to a standstill if women disagree to marry or have children. Babasaheb Ambedkar (1891–1956) enacted various laws for women, including laws for maternity leave, equal pay, suitable working hours, et cetera.

The applicability of feminism to Dalit women is a matter of debate. This is because, in a society that is discriminatory by nature, things like feminism, communalism, colonialism are but obstructions in the way of caste upliftment. Hence, it is a matter of consideration, how much will feminism benefit Dalit women and who will be considered as Dalit women. Moreover, to what extent will Dalit feminism benefit the entire backward Dalit caste or will it create obstacles for the entire Dalit community on their path to progress? So if Dalit women come forward, won't new obstacles be created in the entire social structure as Dalits advance? If that is the case, new doctrines are needed and a rethinking of caste, religion, gender, publication, colonialism, et cetera, is required.

Jyotirao Phule, who had been fighting tirelessly for forty years for the social status and education of women, was deeply moved by the humiliating plight of widows. His last fight in life was to make a strong protest against the custom of tonsuring a widow's head. He had said that if any barber did this, he would be cast out of society. The Satyashodak Samaj published several articles against this cruel practice in the *Deenbandhu* newspaper. Mama Parmanand, a retired politician from Bombay, praised and supported them for these articles. On 14 April 1890, a large meeting of barbers was organised behind the Elphinstone High School which was attended by thousands of barbers, where their leader Sadaba Krishnaji presided and gave a speech that touched many hearts. All the other devotees present at the ceremony admitted that they had committed a sin by tonsuring hapless widows and vowed never to do so again. When the women in London heard the news of this meeting, they sympathised with the plight of Indian widows and supported the declaration made by the barbers. This news was published in *Women Penny*, a London periodical.

If a reservation system for women is put into place, like the reservation system for Dalits, tribals or other backward groups, under which category would the Dalit woman fall—the Dalit category or the women category—is a subject of serious consideration. Moreover, it is also important to consider who would be accepted under the category of Dalit women? Only Dalit women by birth or even the ones who identify themselves under the LGBTQ category? This too, is a matter of consideration to understand if this will hinder the development of Dalit women by birth.

References

Barua, Suparna Lahiri. *Narir Prithibi Narir Songram.*

Chattopadhyay, Debiprasad. *Shey Juge Mayera Boro.*

Haldar, Mahananda. *Sri Sri Guruchand Charit.*

Mallick, Nakul. *Mahatma Jyotirao Phule.*

Sarkar, Kavirasraj Tarakchandra. *Sri Sri Harililamrito.*

Sarkar, Sushma Maitra. *Mon Mukure.*

9

Dalit Women: In Revolutions and Literature

Published in Shramjivi Bhasha, *Volume 8, Number 6, March 2008*, edited by Samudra Dutta.

The role of women who have worked and are working in the area of Dalit literature is not just about composing literary works but also about taking part in activism. This could be within the home or outside. In today's age, Dalit women need to get involved in more social work instead of keeping themselves limited to just writing. There is hardly any presence of Dalit women in Bengal or other provinces in the area of social work. At this point it is necessary to have a cursory—if not a detailed—discussion on the inimitable Savitribai Phule, born almost two hundred years ago, and the work she accomplished despite numerous hurdles. There is such little discussion about Dalit thinkers or extraordinary women that even those scholars in our society who are well-versed in various matters know nothing or hardly feel the need to know anything about them. They don't even consider this as a social responsibility. Even those classmates of mine who teach at universities cannot say a line or two on Babasaheb Ambedkar when asked. Without delving into the subtle politics of not allowing people to read Ambedkar's writings in Bengal and beyond, let us begin with Savitribai Phule.

This person about whom I am going to speak is none other than India's first woman teacher and the pioneer of the Indian women's liberation movement, Savitribai Phule. She was born on 3 January, in the year 1831. The first child of Khandoji Nevase Patil, Savitri was born in Naigaon village which is located in the Satara district of Maharashtra under the Khandala police station, near Shirval.

P. K. Roy says, 'In the thirteenth century, Ramadev Rai Yadav was the king of Devagiri. During his rule, young men from the villages like Siddhakhed, Mahishal, Erul, Chikhalthan, Malthan, etc. served in high ranks of the army. But when the kingdom of Devagiri fell, the well-to-do clans of Nevase, Panchore, Yadav, Raut, etc., were left in dire straits.'

As far as it is known, the Nevase clan has enjoyed a high position from the time of Shivaji to the Peshwa period. For this reason, they have graced the position of the village head (Mukhiya Patel) of Naigaon. In Naigaon, there were very few people from communities other than the Mali community. Khandoji used to donate a part of his earnings for the welfare of the underprivileged.

At the early age of nine, Savitribai Phule got married to Jyotiba Phule. Jyotiba was only thirteen years old at that time, in 1840. During the same year, the British established the Normal School. After completing his primary education, Jyotiba was forced to drop out of school because of the Manuvadis.[1] He turned his focus to farming. Sitting in the

---

[1] The Manuvadis are the supporters of *Manusmriti*, an ancient Hindu text known for its rigid caste-based social norms. The Manuvadis often upheld discriminatory practices against marginalised communities, particularly against women and Dalits, limiting their access to education and other opportunities.

shade of the mango orchard while working on his farm, he unfurled the flag of women's education and became the first person to initiate female education in India. He started with his first two students, his maternal cousin Sagunabai Kshirsagar and wife Savitribai. After working hard on his field from morning to noon, he would sit down to give them lessons in math and other primary subjects.

Jyotiba was sent back to school again at the age of fourteen. He completed his education in an English medium school in 1847. He realised that female education was much more important than male education. In 1848, Jyotiba established the first school for girls at Bhideji's house[2] or 'wada' in Pune and struck a blow against the prejudices of the prevailing social system. The British had opened a school in Pune in 1832. Parents were required to bring a letter from the District Magistrate to get their children admitted to that school. With the help of Munshiji, Jyotiba managed to collect a letter from the District Magistrate and thereby succeeded in getting Sagunabai admitted to that school. If one's name was registered in that school, they could study and appear for the exams in due course of time. Jyotiba, in the meantime, continued teaching Savitribai and Sagunabai.

The founder of Normal School was Mrs Mitchell. She was the wife of Reverend Mitchell. She had deep sympathy for women's education. She gave Saguna and Savitri their third-class certificates. At that time, the third class signified the eighth grade. The Normal School, which was established in 1840 in the house of Chhabil Das, gradually progressed. This is where Savitri and Saguna completed their education. During this time, Savitri became particularly active in the women's liberation movement after reading the biography of Thomas Clarkson. She learnt that in 1785, Clarkson was a student at Cambridge University. She also learnt that the

---

[2] Tatya Saheb Bhide.

white-skinned people of America considered the black-skinned people of Africa to be slaves or like animals. They were subjected to inhuman treatment. Clarkson raised his voice against this injustice. He was the first leader to fight for Black people's demands for human rights. Ushering in victory through agitation, he succeeded in forcing the government to pass laws in favour of Black people.

Phule encouraged both Savitri and Saguna to devote their life to teaching. Savitri started teaching in the school that was set up in Bhideji's house. She thus became the first woman teacher of modern India. Jointly with her husband, she engaged in various social service activities. These included the establishment of schools by Christian missionaries, setting up hospitals, providing food to famine victims, helping 'fallen' women and caring for orphans.

The second girls' school was established at Rasta Peth on 18 September 1851. The same year, on 16 October, the students of the school established by Savitri and Jyotiba had the opportunity to sit for their first examination. On 15 March 1852, a third girls' school was inaugurated at Budhwar Peth.

Among Savitribai's other works is the construction of infanticide prevention houses. This organisation helped save the lives of many unwanted innocent children. On 24 September 1873, the Satyashodhak Samaj was founded in Pune amidst a grand ceremony. Sixty social workers and intellectuals were present there.

The objectives of the Satyashodhak Samaj were as follows: (1) modest rituals; (2) compulsory education; (3) use of swadeshi products; (4) marriage rituals by non-brahmins; (5) freeing people from the fear of astrology, ghosts and imaginary demons; (6) abolition of casteism and idol worship; and (7) spreading awareness that all scriptures including the Vedas, Quran and Bible, are man's creation, not God's.

In 1876 there was a famine in Maharashtra. At that time, the Phule couple stood with those affected by the famine.

Savitri took on the responsibility of accommodating two thousand students of the Satyashodhak Samaj and built a hostel.

In an age when the heads of widows were tonsured, Savitribai protested against the system and formed an organisation consisting of barbers. This was the first association of barbers in the history of India. On 18 July 1880, Savitri and Jyotiba participated in the protest against the licensing of liquor shops. In 1883, Jyotiba Phule wrote a book advocating the interest of farmers called *Shetkaryaca Asud* ('The Whipcord of the Cultivators').

On the subject of widow remarriage, Savitri organised a fifteen-day ceremony for widows. It was the first women's meeting by the women involved in India's women's liberation movement. In her written works, Savitribai Phule sings the song of liberation of women and shudras. Her works include *Kavya Phule* (1854), *Bavan Kashi Subodh Ratnakar, Bharatmata - Collection of Savitribai's Lectures and Songs,* Jyotiba's lectures, various speeches by Savitribai Phule, and two letters written for Jyotiba by Savitribai.

Something needs to be said about the other women in Maharashtra who joined Babasaheb Ambedkar's movement. There was Ramabai (Ambedkar's wife), who silently supported Babasaheb throughout her life. When Babasaheb was teaching abroad, she toiled making cowdung cakes, to douse her hunger. She lost a child due to lack of medical care. On 20 July 1924, when Babasaheb organised a drive to build schools and hostels at Dalit settlement areas and started an anti-untouchability movement under the banner of Bahishkrit Hitakarani Sabha, she joined him. At that time Keshubai Bhatkar and Rangubai Subhakar played significant roles. Both of them were good speakers and singers.

In a similar fashion, Jaibai Chaudhary from Nagpur started the Chokhamela Kanya Paathshala in 1924. Initially, the school was attended by only four students. Gradually, the numbers rose and the school was converted into a college. Tulsibai Bansode started a newspaper titled *Chokhamela*. Her daughter Rajashree, directed a three-hour film on Ambedkar. She also founded the Dalit women's Samata Sainik Dal.

A large number of women participated in Babasaheb's Mahad Satyagraha on 20 March 1927. On 13 November of that year, a meeting was organised at Amaravati on the occasion of the Temple Entry Movement. The movement saw participation by a large number of women. On 25 December 1927, Babasaheb burnt the *Manusmriti*. In January 1928, the Mahila Mandal of Mumbai was established under the presidency of Ramabai Ambedkar.

In 1936, Babasaheb raised his voice against the devadasi practice. Ambedkar was joined in 1920 by Radhabai Kamble, who was a labour leader in the cotton mills.

The proposals adopted by Babasaheb at various sessions conducted by him, are as follows:

1. Making education compulsory for women
2. Women's representation in local administration and regional assemblies
3. Stick-wielding and self-defence training for untouchable women
4. Establishing a woman's branch of the Samata Sainik Dal
5. Prohibition of child marriages, et cetera.

On 20 July 1942, Babasaheb established the Akhil Bharatiya Anusuchit Jati Mahasangh in Nagpur. Twenty-five thousand women were present at this session. This session was chaired by Sulochona Bhogre and the main secretary was Indira Patil.

At that time it was difficult for Dalit students to enter college. That's why Babasaheb established the People's Education Society. This society was established in Mumbai and Aurangabad. Anjanabhai Deshabrata established a hostel in 1924 in Nagpur and Jayabai Chaudhary established one for students in Nasik. The event where Babasaheb converted to Buddhism (14 October 1956), was attended by many women.

Among other female writers from Maharashtra, we have Shantabai Kamble. Her autobiography *Majya Jalmachi Chittarkatha* was published in 1988. There is also Kumud Pawde's autobiography *Jina Amucha* and Urmila Pawar's autobiography *Aidan* ('Weave'). Urmila was born in 1954. Her works include *Sahar Bot*, *Chauthi Bhint*, *Hatcha Ek*, *Udan*, *Doan Ekankika*.

Marathi Dalit poet Jyotir Lanjwar was born in 1950. Her poetry has been translated into English.

The Tamil writer Bama is extremely well known. She was born in 1985. She belongs to the Paraya community. Her autobiography is titled *Karukku*, and among the other works she has written are *Sangati*, *Vanman*, *Manuci*, *Kusumbukkaran*, *Oru Tattavum Erumaiyum*, *Kondattam*, and others.

Among others, P. Sivakami is a very powerful writer. In her essays, the topic of feminism reaches new heights. A small excerpt from her essay 'Land: Women's Breath and Speech' is enough to give the core idea of feminism. She says, 'At a time when it is argued that feminism is synonymous with body politics, the argument that feminism means—sharing land and resources—must also blossom. Land must be a subject of debate in women's discussions and writings. The third revolution is women's liberation which is centred on land' (280).

Another writer is S. Sukirtharani, with her sharp-edged poetry. Born in 1973, Sukirta's mother is Christian and her father is of the lower-caste Parachi community. Her collection of poetry includes *Kaipattri Yen Kanavu Kel, Iravu Mirugam, Avalai Mozhipeyarthal, Theendapadaatha Muttham*, et cetera.

Recently, Lakshmi M.'s autobiography won the Sparrow Literary Award. Cobin Maller, born in the seventies, is the author of this generation. Eranga Mallika is a poet and essayist.

Gujarati writer Chandraben Shrimali was born in 1950. She is the author of three poetry collections, three short story collections, and one novel. She belongs to the Garda caste. She crafts her short stories with great dexterity.

Kannada writer D. U. Saraswati was born in 1963. She is a writer, poet and short story writer from the Madiga community. Her short stories bring out the extraordinary flavour of Dalit public life. Theatre worker and philanthropist Saraswati's books of poetry and other works include *Henedare Jedananthe, Jeeva Sampige*, and *Eegen Maadeeri*.

Telugu writer Jupekka Subhadra was born in 1964. *Ayyayyo Dammakka* is her poetry collection, and *Makka/Mukka Pulla Genne* her collection of short stories. She belongs to the Madiga community.

Now I will shed some light on female writers from Bengal. Among them, Sushma Maitra Sarkar's name always comes to the fore. Sushma was born in the month of Magh (the tenth month in the Bengali calendar) in 1929 in Bethuria, a barely-known village near Gopalganj Orakandi in Faridpur district. While putting up at the Thakur residence in Orakandi, she passed her IA[3] exams in 1944 from Ramdia Srikrishna College. At that time, she was teaching at Shanti

---

[3] The IA (Intermediate of Arts) was a pre-university examination equivalent to the first two years of college education after high school, usually taken before pursuing a bachelor's degree. This system was prevalent in India and other South Asian countries during the early- to mid-twentieth century.

Satya Bhama Balika Vidyalaya at the Thakur residence. Guruchand Thakur treated her with great affection. In 1946, when Dr Ambedkar was disheartened after losing all chances of entering the Constituent Assembly by getting elected from Maharashtra, the big-hearted Jogendranath Mandal—the perpetual leader of the Bengal branch of the All India Scheduled Castes Federation—assured him of a seat from Bengal. For this reason, along with representatives on behalf of the women's organisation like Santosh Kumari Talukdar, Bina Samaddar, Swarnalata Hazra, Pritilata Halder, Prabhati Biswas, Kamal Bagchi, Shefali Biswas, and others, he bowed down before various political personalities. Sushma's first story 'Harprasad' was published in *Pravasi* in 1969. A detailed understanding of her various activities might be needed.

In 1971, she devoted herself to the service of millions of refugees who were victims of the Bangladesh Liberation War. Under the leadership of Apurba Lal Majumdar and Charumihir Sarkar, she formed the Bangladesh Sharanarthi and Mukti Sangram Sahayok Samiti. She also established the Ambedkar Free Primary School in 1975 for the education of neglected boys and girls from the Paikpara area. Currently it is being managed with government assistance.

Further, she was integral in championing movements and forming public opinion against the government's injustice and oppression of the refugees who were dislocated from Marichjhapi in 1978. The reason behind providing so much detail about her is because there is so little discussion about her activities that it seems necessary to give a basic introduction to them.

A collection of essays written by her has been compiled in *Mon Mukure*, along with essays related to her activities. Among her other works are *Onyoswad: Onyorong*, *Ek Ekke Ek*, *Mahiyashi Shyamohini*, *Ram Goyalar Sworgolabh*, *Markin Bidushi Mahila*, *Bahni*, *Amader Maa*, and *Banglar*

Virangana.
Bina Ray Sarkar was born in 1940 in Bikrampur's Ranagram, Dhaka. Books written by her include *Deepshika, Jago Nari Jago, Asha-Nirashar Kotha*, et cetera.

Srimati Kiran Talukdar was born in 1945 at Kaliyagop village which comes under the Jhalokathi police station in Barishal district. Her research articles include, 'Biswa Mahamandale Matuadharma', 'Jannayok Mukundobihari Mallick—Jibon o Sadhona', 'Kabirmanishi', and 'Biswakobi o Kobirmanish'. Her book of poetry is *Shantir Pothe*.

Manju Bala was born in 1954 at Naliakhali in Canning, South 24 Parganas. Adept at both verse and prose, Manju was the editor of the *Ekhon Tokhon* magazine. Her books of poetry include *Churno Samudrer Dheu*, and *Oswarohir Opekkhyay*. *Chorabali* is her collection of short stories, and *Uttoron* her book of plays.

Lily Halder was born on 6 September, 1957, in Kasba, South Kolkata. Lily, an MA in Political Science and a retired railway worker, has to her credit the following collections of poems: *Purnogrash, Nimphooler Gondho, Rakhaler Landscape*, and others.

Smritikona Howlader was born on 29 April 1960, in Sahebganj, Jharkhand. The *Jan-Jagaran* magazine was published under her editorship. Adept at Dalit poetry and music, Smritikona has to her credit the book of poetry *Borne Borne Mormo Kotha*.

Chuni Kotal was born in 1965 in Goaldihi near Shalbani in West Medinipur. Continuous caste-based harassment forced her to commit suicide on 16 August 1992. Some of her writings can be found scattered here and there. It has been published in periodicals like *Chaturtha Duniya, Neer*, and *Sundor*. Her writing has been published in *Neer*'s special issue on short autobiographies of Dalit women.

Among others who have written since the late-1980s, noteworthy names are Lakshmi Mandi, Pallabi Mandal,

Ashalata Ray, Kanan Baral, Alaknanda Roy, Kanika Sarkar, Sujata Biswas, Saptadwipa Adhikary, and Ila Das.

The intellectuals of Bengal have always been terribly silent about Dalit writings and great Dalit personalities. Not only that, they have not stepped back from erasing leaders like Jogendranath Mandal from the pages of history. So why would they care for the apparently insignificant work coming from Dalit women? However, even if at a slow pace, Dalit girls from Bengal are doing some great work. I don't know when it will be appreciated. But let's hope this work will continue.

References

Bandhyopadhyay, Debasis, ed. *Journal of the Department of English*, Vidyasagar University.

Charal, Kalyani Thakur, ed. *Neer Ritupatra* (special issue on essays by Dalit women).

Charal, Kalyani Thakur, ed. *Neer Ritupatra* (special issue on poems by Dalit women).

Roy, Debesh. *Dalit-Sankalan Sampadana*.

Roy, P. K. *Mayiyashi Nari Savitribai Phule*.

Sarkar, Sushma Maitra. *Mon Mukure*.

Sivakami, P. "Land: Women's Breath and Speech". *The Oxford India Anthology of Tamil Dalit Writing*, edited by Ravikumar and R. Azhagarasan.

Tripathi, Kusum. *Antaranga Sangeeti-Sampadak Dibya Jaina (Ambedkarbadi Dalit Mahila Andolan ka Mulyankan)*.

Scan the QR code to hear Kalyani Thakur Charal read the works of some of the women poets discussed in this essay.

10

A Few Dalit Women in Bengali Literature and Music

Published in Neer Ritupatra, *20th Issue, 3 February 2021.*

In the history of Bengali literature, writing that comes under the title of 'Dalit women's writing' have hardly been observed from the initial phase. The artists or lyric-poets from Dalit families that can be found after a thorough search include Sulochona—the lyric poet from Mymensingh; Kamini Sundari—the Royani artist; Rami—the poet of Krishna Leela; Anantabala Vaishnabi—the Vaishnava Padavali singer; and from the present age Sudhamukhi Goswami and Sushma Maitra Sarkar, et cetera, who are among the especially notable names. There may have been many other oral poets and artists about whom I too have no idea.

Sulochona

Sulochona, the composer of *Sri Sri Gopini Kirtan* has been mentioned in Dinesh Chandra Sen's *Mymensingh Gitika*.[1] The daughter of an illiterate Chandala family, Sulochona

---

[1] A collection of folk ballads, all sourced from the region of Myemensingh, Bangladesh.

was born in 1776. Her father's name was Ramdev. She was married off at a young age. Sulochona's father Ramdev had plans of keeping Jayhari, Sulochona's husband, as a live-in son-in-law after offering his daughter to him in marriage. For quite some time, he lived at his wife's place as the family's jamai or son-in-law, but worldly bonds were not sufficient to keep him captive. One day, behind everyone's back, he left his father-in-law's abode never to be found again.

Sulochona's life is the life of a lonely, jilted lover. The lonely Sulochona simply wanted to express her pain in words. But she wasn't literate yet. She came to know about a male teacher from the neighbouring village by the name of Chorunath. She went to meet him after a great deal of mental preparation. She wrote,

> *Chorunaather paaye bondi lutaiyaa dhoraa*
> *Haatein dhori je more shikhaaila lekhaporaa.*[2]

She further wrote,

> *Ogyaanetey chilaam aami ondher shomaan.*
> *Doya kori dila guru meliya noyaan.*[3]

She lived a long life and died at the age of ninety. As long as her parents were alive, she lived at her paternal place in Thakurkona (Mymensingh district) with her brothers Roba and Dukhiya. After the death of her parents, she went to live in the neighbouring village Chhatrashal at her nephew's house. There was a special reason for her relocating to Chhatrashal. Chorunath, the teacher who introduced her to the world of letters, was a former teacher at the Chhatrashal village school. Sulochona not only showed her skills in her high-level musical pursuits, she also strove hard to prove

---

[2] The girl fell down at the feet of Chorunath, requesting him to educate her.
[3] I was living like a blind person, when my guru presented me with a new vision.

her dexterity as a creator of literary works. In the last few years of her life, this was her priority.

Rami-Tara or Ramtara

There is much debate about the date of composition and the name of the composer of *Sri Krishna Kirtan*.[4] Sukumar Sen notes that, 'Jayananda's *Chaitanyamangal* mentions Chandidas as an ancient poet. Jayananda mentions the name of Chandidas, right after Jayadeva and Vidyapati, as the composer of the Krishnacharit verses or Padavali.'

Jayadeva, Vidyapati aar Chandidaas
Srikrishnacharitra tara korilo prokaash.[5]

Here, the word 'tara' (which usually means 'they' in Bengali) has not been used in the usual sense but as a reference to Rajakini Rami or Rami the washerwoman, who was also known as 'Tara' or 'Ramtara'. 'The composer of the *Sri Krishna Kirtan* has introduced himself as Badu Chandidas throughout,' says Sen.

He adds that more than two-thirds of the songs in *Sri Krishna Kirtan* comprise hymns on the Basali goddesses—Basali Bandi, Basalibore, Basaligon, Basaligeeti, Basali Ayee, et cetera. Boru and Basali suggest that the poet of the *Sri Krishna Kirtan* was a devotee of goddess Basali and an attendant in charge of a particular domain for the seva-puja[6] at the Basali shrine.

Sukumar Sen has written,

> 'Badu' = 'Dwij' (Elder). People who believe this, consider Dwij Chandidas of *Vaishnava Padavali* to be the same person as Badu Chandidas. However, 'Badu' and 'Dwij' are not always synonymous. In Odisha and Assam (even

---

[4] This is a genre of devotional music.
[5] Jaydev, Vidyapati, and Chandidas brought out the *Sri Krishna Charit*.
[6] The daily worship rituals.

in Bengal), 'Badu' refers to the non-brahmin castes. There is no reason to think that the author of *Sri Krishna Kirtan* was not a Dalit writer. (125–27)

Firstly, the poet's name was Chandidas and he was a temple servant at the Basali Devi shrine. Basali is not an Aryan goddess. Secondly, the poet's name was Ananta and he was a devotee and a temple servant of the goddess Chandi (synonymous with Basali). Hence, he had taken the name of Badu Chandidas. Thirdly, the identity 'Ananta' is a later interpolation.

'The story of Chandidas and his lover, a washerwoman (variously named Tara, Ramtara, Rami) dates back to the seventeenth century. Chandidas's lover is from the lower caste, so can it really be boldly asserted that Badu Chandidas is from a higher caste?' (125–27).

Chandidas's Prakriti (female counterpart/muse) was the washerwoman (aka Neta). Both the queen and the princess evade the reach of history. However, Lakhima is mentioned in some of the introductory verses or bhanitas of Vidyapati; the washerwoman appears in some verses and legends.

'Chandidas was a puppeteer and had a puppet theatre in Kanai-Natshal village near Gaur,' says Sen. Rami's story has not been discussed as much as Chandidas's story.

There are many debates around Chandidas, whether it is Badu Chandidas, Dwij Chandidas, Dino Chandidas, Taruni-Raman Chandidas, et cetera. There are different stories about Chandidas. In *Bangla Sahityer Ruprekha* ('The Outline of Bengali Literature'), Gopal Halder has written,

> But there is another story—the poet was in love with a washerwoman—her name was Rami or Tara or Ramtara. And this love was in the Sahajiya tradition. "Pure gold, with not even a whiff of sexual love"—established in its own grandeur by disdaining society's frown. There are Sahajiya verses in Rami's name too as there are Rami's dhyans in Chandidas's name along with piriter joygan or songs of romance. Needless to say this is the creation of

the Sahajiyas.⁷ When Chandidas became the property of all of Bengali society, why would the Sahajiyas abandon their claim on him?

The Empress of Royani, Kamini Sundari

Kamini Devi was born in the year 1885 (the Bengali year 1292) in Katakhali village of Pirojpur police station, Barisal district. Her father was Feduram Byapari and mother was Durgamani. Her father, Fedu, was an extremely simple-minded person. People used to call him 'Byapari' as he used to trade in earthenware. Their paternal surname was Roy. Due to the lack of schools nearby, Kamini Devi was not able to acquire an education. In any case, women were not allowed to be educated in those ages. However, she had a sharp memory ever since she was a little girl. Any song, poem, shloka or story that she had heard once, she could recite from memory. Kamini herself was a truly desirable woman. Enamoured by her beauty, the wealthy Ashwini singer of Pirojpur took a liking towards her and got her married to his eldest son, Haradhan. Kamini Devi got married at the tender age of eleven, in the Bengali year 1303. On the night of her wedding, alone in her wedding room, she started humming lines from the song 'Jole dheu diyo na, jole dheu diyo na, olo pransokhi' ('Don't make waves in the water, O soul companion). Everyone was surprised to hear Kamini's melodious voice.

Her idyllic life was disrupted after two years and eight months of her marriage—in the Bengali year 1306. Darkness descended on her life. She lost her husband when a tree fell on him and killed him. Unable to bear the torture at her in-laws' place, Kamini moved back to her father's house. Rajchandra Sikdar of Pirojpur's Shimuliya village

---

⁷ An esoteric religious cult that drew a parallel between human and divine love.

was her distant relative. He used to run small jatra groups,[8] as well as Royani[9] singing troupes. He was not only a skilled director but also a great singer.

Rajchandra Sikdar requested Kamini to join his Royani troupe as a singer. He told her family, 'Either get your daughter married, or let her join my group.' Her mother Durgamani asked Kamini to join the Royani singing group. She was then sixteen. Rajchandra Sikdar created a new Royani singing group. At the performances, Kamini's wave-like voice would resonate with a melodious tone. It was as if the genre of Royani singing was riding on high tides. The audiences would throw handkerchiefs stuffed with money at her. Her name and fame spread everywhere. There were multiple invitations for her performances. She was invited to places beyond Barishal, like Khulna and Faridpur. She was showered with awards. Money worth five or ten rupees, brassware, silver medals, gold medals, gold pendants, gold necklaces, and others started coming in as rewards.

Rajchandra Sikdar suddenly passed away because of old age. Kamini was around twenty-three or twenty-four years old then. She took over the responsibility of the group. People refer to it as a revolution in the domain of theatre and music. She built a grand budgerow and included more women in the group. Previously, during Royani singing, only one person would sing during the dramatisation of the *Manashamangal Kavya*. Later, other characters began to be staged. Costumes were created similar to that of a jatra. Along with this, Kamini added music from patriotic songs, kobiyali and kirtan. Sets were created of Behula's wedding room, Hetal's lathi, a banana raft, et cetera. It was just like the first generation of modern theatre. A revolution had

---

[8] Popular form of folk-theatre from Bengal.
[9] Royani is a folk ritual theatre based on oral renditions of *Manashamangal Kavya*, narrating the resurrection of Lakshindar and the worship of Goddess Manasa.

come in the domain of Royani singing. With that came dignity, wide-ranging fame, prestige, recognition and affluence into her life.

Since she had not had access to education, she made sure to admit her only daughter and nephews and nieces to schools and even arranged for home-tutors for them.

After her father's death, she was not able to throw a feast for her relatives. She decided to feed brahmins along with her own relatives. Both sides—the Namashudras as well as the brahmins—objected to this. Later, she organised the event with the help of Narayan Putatunda, a brahmin. At that time, Putatunda pointed out in front of thirty-six Namashudra chiefs: 'When Kamini Sundari staged her *Manashamangal Kavya*, everybody including the Hindus, the Muslims, the shudras, would bow down to her feet. Everybody took the water from the pitcher in her hand as holy water. Then what is the objection against joining her celebrations?' Later on, she married her brother off in the Vedic tradition, which was not permitted for the shudras and atishudras.

Kamini Sundari was a feminist. Through the *Manashamangal Kavya*, she spread the wave of women's liberation. She taught the Royani style of singing to many women. It was her efforts that led to the formation of twelve Royani groups in Bengal.

When Kamini Sundari grew older, people from all the caste groups in the area decided to give due respect to the great Royani artist. Twelve women's artist groups participated in this event. The event went on for seven days. In the end, the chairperson of the committee of judges announced the name of the best Royani artist. Shrimati Aayna secured the third position, Shrimati Labanya the second, and Shrimati Kamini Sundari the first.

Because of Partition and the communal riots, she had to move to the Indian state of West Bengal. She lived in the

Mamudpur Colony of 24 North Paraganas. She passed away in the Bengali year 1364 (1957 by the Gregorian calendar).

Anantabala Vaishnabi

She was born in the Bengali year 1290, on the fourteenth of Phalgun, a Tuesday. Her father was Tarinicharan Gayen. They were from Turuk-Khali village, the present Purbasachiya, in Barishal district. Her parents had given her the name Harashundari. When she was young, everyone called her Haro. They had another house in Chaigharaiya village in the same area. The Beluya River flowed next to it. The Chaigharaiya house was known as the old house and the one at Turuk-Khali was the new house. Turuk-Khali was a wetland. As soon as the rainy season arrived, the fields would overflow with water. There was no other way to travel save for boats. Till the time she left the country, Harashundari spent her life at both the houses. Anantabala's life was filled with the sounds of the fields, the rivers, the trees, and the canals of this rural environment. The singer's family surname was Gayen. Maybe one of her ancestors had acquired this surname through singing. Harashundari's grandfather could sing. Harashundari's father too used to sing beautiful polligeeti, bhatiyali, kirtan, dehatattva, et cetera.[10]

If there was a kirtan or Harir Lut, or any other big festival in the neighbouring villages, Tarini Gayen would be summoned. He would take his children along. Among Tarinibabu's three sons—Jogeshchandra, Umeshchandra and Ganeshchandra—Umesh and Ganesh were good

---

[10] Polligeeti, bhatiyali, kirtan, and dehatattva are integral to Bengali folk music. Polligeeti represents lok-sangeet, while bhatiyali is sung by boatmen on rivers. Kirtan involves devotional storytelling in Indian religions, and dehatattva, popular among Bauls, explores spiritual themes, reflecting Bengal's deep-rooted musical and philosophical traditions.

singers. They had a separate kirtan group. They had also formed a group which would sing from the *Ramayana*. Some years, just before Neel pujo, they would go singing songs from one village to the other in groups of eight.

In her childhood, Harashundari would accompany her father for Harir Lut or Kirtan Mahotsav. Wherever she went, she would captivate the crowd by playing the gopiyantra.[11]

Harashundari got married at the age of seven. She was taken away against a meagre bride price of thirty rupees. The marriage, however, was not a happy one. She lost her husband in a few years. After this, the artist spent her life in many ways, singing here and there. Once, she even went for a Royani performance. She would be invited to sing at various events at the village, like the women's festival Uthoni, Tarar Broto, and others. Those songs were, of course, a choral performance by women. They were created orally. For instance,

> *Kaake kore kolorob*
> *Kokiler dhoni*
> *Pohailo rajani.*[12]

Or,

> *Kaalaa amaay pagol korli re*
> *Ghore roi kemone*[13]

Harashundari would sing while sorting rice grains with her feet. She would even be scolded by her mother for singing while cooking.

---

[11] A kind of musical instrument.
[12] One can hear the crows clamouring and the cuckoos calling. The night is over.
[13] Here 'Kala' (which means black) is a reference to Krishna, portrayed in all cultural representations as possessing dark skin. The speaker is possibly Radha, his chief consort. She expresses her feeling of being restless at home, when music from Krishna's flute is filtering in.

Despite great love and affection from her parents, the artist continued to struggle mentally. Sleep evaded her in the night. One day she left for Kolkata thinking she could make a name for herself if she went there. From the Matibhanga wharf, she boarded a ship and reached Khulna. From there, she took a vehicle directly to Kolkata. After leaving her country, Harashundari converted to Vaishnavism. She gave up the name given to her by her parents and adopted the new name of Anantabala. From that day onwards, she came to be known as Vaishnabi Anantabala.

After reaching Kolkata, the artist stayed at Haridas Bairagi's house at 74 Haldar Pukur Lane, Salkia, Howrah. This was the Bengali year 1337. She hadn't been able to bring much money from her home and had to rely on begging. She would beg for alms, singing from neighbourhood to neighbourhood. This is how her days passed. One day, like she usually did, she was singing and begging on the streets when a boy came and asked her, 'If I pay you some advance money, will you sing?'

Anantabala raised her face. She was amazed to know that people would pay money to hear her sing. When the boy asked again, she immediately agreed. The name of this boy was Ismail. Ismail took down her address and arrived at her residence the next day. Giving her an advance of ten rupees, he took Anantabala as a singer to a function organised by the Shalimar Company. There, she was introduced to a sailor from a boat. His name was Mangal Fakir. At the event, Fakir sang in the guru dhara and Anantabala in the shishyo dhara.[14]

---

[14] In this context, the guru (spiritual guide) and shishyo (disciple) bhab-dhara is a particular style of Bengali folk singing that unfolds as a musical dialogue or debate between two singers. This genre, common in Baul and other folk traditions, features one performer as a teacher or spiritual guide (guru) and the other as a seeker or disciple (shishya). Their exchange, often philosophical or spiritual, is marked by improvisation, call-and-response singing, and deep emotional expression.

Usually these musical sessions were jam-packed with an enthusiastic crowd. That day, Anantabala and Fakir Saheb's event also turned out to be the same way. Fakir Saheb liked Anantabala's singing so much that he started referring to her as his daughter acquired through faith. From that day onwards, Anantabala started calling Fakir Saheb her father.

Somed Saheb was present at the event. He was the driver of a senior official at His Masters' Voice (HMV). His house was in Dhaka. He told Anantabala, 'Tomorrow you will come with me. I want to see if we can make you sing "Koler Gaan"'.[15]

The next day, Anantabala went with Somed Saheb. However, instead of taking the artist to HMV, he took her to Jitendranath Ghosh Dastidar, who was the owner of the Megaphone Company. He was very impressed with Anantabala's singing and arranged for rehearsals from the very next day itself.

Jitenbabu had another name, which was Mega. Hence, his company was named Megaphone. This company was established in 1910. In the beginning, the company used to sell gramophones. They were also wholesale suppliers of gramophone records. They started the business of record production in 1934.

HMV was owned by a foreigner. He was not interested in the country's folk music, polligeeti or kirtan. Among the other record companies (Somela, Hindustan, Pioneer, Colombia, et cetera.), none had tried to project gems from the Indian artistic scene like Megaphone. No other company had such a crowd of debut singers or Vaishnav-Vaishnavis emerge under their label. Apart from Anantabala, the other Vaishnav-Vaishnavis included Lolita Vaishnabi, Kamini Vaishnabi, Nanibala Vaishnabi, Horidasi Vaishnabi, Bhabani Vaishnab, Swarupdas Vaishnab, et cetera. Jitenbabu had created the space for them to sing.

---

[15] Gramophone song.

Anantabala's first record was released in 1937. However, it seems that the lines of the first song that she recorded were:

> Amaar praan kande bhaaire soday maiya bole
> Holo maiyate utpotti jogot
> Maiya amaar hridi dole
> Maiyar guner ki dei seema
> Dwapor juge Krishnaleela -
> Koren shei kaalaa -
> Je din giri dhaaron korlen Krishne -
> Shedin shaktirupe sonchaarile [16]

Gyan Datta from Barishal was her guru for the first song, even though technically at that stage she mainly sang polligeeti by ear rather than through formal training. Her next guru was Shri Paresh Deb. Megaphone had hired Pareshbabu just to train Anantabala to sing. Pareshbabu had also rendered the accompanying music to many of Anantabala's songs. Anantabala had also taken music lessons from Kavi Nazrul. The singer had recorded two of Nazrul's compositions, which had also been released in the market. However, no trace of these records can be found anymore.

Before Anantabala entered the gramophone singing market with polligeeti, there had been only one polligeeti by Abbasuddin which had been brought out by HMV. The first few lines of that song were 'Amar harkala korlam re duronto porobashi'. At that point of time, the term polligeeti was still not in use. But bhatiyali gaan was. Megaphone had handed over the bhatiyali section to Anantabala. Out

---

[16] The song conveys a deep reverence for the divine feminine, portraying her as the source of all creation and an immeasurable force. It alludes to the idea that divine acts of power are sustained by an unseen cosmic energy, highlighting an intrinsic connection between spiritual strength and a greater, transcendental presence.

of all the bhatiyali records, almost 60 per cent were in Anantabala's voice.

Society's perception about women who were gramophone singers was not very good. Later this perception changed. Meanwhile, Angurbala, Ascharyamoyi Devi, Indubala, Indulekha, Kamla Jhoriya, Harimati Debi, and other singers had already dismantled this unfair outlook practised by society. Anantabala was the undisputed empress of bhatiyali–polligeeti singing among the other female singers of that time.

Other than Anantabala Vaishnabi, no other Vaishnavite has recorded Islamiya music.[17] In 1937, she brought out the first Islamiya music record. Whenever the topic of Bengali Islamiya music comes up, the first person who is remembered with respect is Abbasuddin. If any name comes after that, it is that of Kavi Nazrul. The third memorable name in this genre of music is of course that of Anantabala. On one side we find Abbasuddin, and Anantabala on the other.

Apart from Abbasuddin and Anantabala, the other Islamiya music singers of that era were Gani Miyan, Delowar Hossain, Sona Miyah, Sakina Begam, Amina Begum, Rabeya Khatun, Luthfounnisa, Master Somen Ali, Abdul Latif, Nuruddin Ahmed, Mohammad Qasem, Mohammad Arfan Ali, Gulam Mustafa, and Takrim Ahmed. Abbasuddin himself had created opportunities for Takrim Ahmed and Ghulam Mustafa. Among these singers, the first five sang under pseudonyms. Their original names are Dhiren Das, Chitta Roy, Girin Chakraborty, Ascharyamoyi Debi, and Harimati Debi respectively.

One particular Islamiya song sung by Anantabala became immensely popular. It sold five hundred records in two days. The record number was J.N.G. 5053.

---

[17] Islamiya music is a genre of Bengali bhakti geeti that is more free-flowing in structure than a ghazal.

Dhoni prem korte paarbi ki tora
Amaar nur nodi jogoter poti
Premete se holo koraa
Premer totto jene nobi dhore aane choddo bibi
Ter pay naa munshi maulvi jaananaa.[18]

After listening to the song, a young Jasim Uddin brought the recording to the notice of the elder Maulana Sahib of Kushtia and said that the phrase 'choddo bibi' (fourteen wives) reflects aspects of Shari'ah (divine law), making such usage sinful. After listening to the song, the elder Maulana Sahib sent a letter to Anantabala through the record company. The main argument of the letter was that the song could run if the phrase 'choddo bibi' was replaced by 'egaro bibi' (eleven wives). Jitenbabu and the singer jointly decided that the song would be re-recorded by making the said changes and they informed the Maulana Sahib. The moment Jasim Uddin got to know about the letter, he filed a case at the Kushtia court saying that the use of 'choddo bibi' in the song was against Islam and that a Hindu woman cannot sing Islamic songs. This case dragged on for a year. The company lost the case in the end. The police came and broke the records of this song.

Anantabala has recorded almost two hundred songs. However, many of them cannot be traced anymore. She has enthralled people by singing a wide variety of genres like polligeeti, gramya geeti, gramyo sangeet, bhatiyali, kirtan, Islamiya, et cetera.

All her records were damaged because of Partition. These songs would sometimes play on the radio. She herself retained none of them in her possession. She spent her last days near the Krishnanagar Road Station, in a house with a

---

[18] The song explores divine love through Prophet Muhammad (Nur Nabi), portraying love as transcending material wealth and scholarly understanding. It suggests that true love, both spiritual and worldly, is beyond the grasp of religious authorities.

thatched roof and jute-wood fence. One of her songs, 'Nimai dara re...'[19] can transfix listeners. Anantabala spent her last few days in the very same country where Nimai was born.

Sudhamukhi Goswami

Here, it must be said that we get the genre of Dalit women's autobiographical writing from Sudhamukhi Goswami's autobiography *Atmajibonir Moto*. The problem is that Sudhamukhi was not the sole writer of the book. *Atmajibonir Moto* is found within the same cover as the book *Obor Belar Paari*, her husband Banamali Goswami's autobiography. Perhaps this is the reason why the book escapes everyone's attention. The book mainly covers the subject of how a Dalit girl has to struggle to acquire education and start a career, along with the regional history of the two countries. We find the history of the formation of various schools in the Jessore–Khulna region of Egarokhan, Maliat, Maslahati, et cetera, from Banamali Goswami's *Obor Belar Paari*. Sudhamukhi Goswami's autobiography is filled with stories from her own life, and more than that, her family's story.

She writes,

> It might not be too offensive to call the age that I was born in as the dark era. That period was characterised by its superstitious mentality and lack of education. I was born in that age of ignorance, in the Bengali month of Ashwin of the year 1316 (October 1909 of the English calendar). That year in Ashwin, a violent storm raged through East Bengal. For that reason my mother remembered my birth month, although not the dates.

Sudhamukhi was born in Hidia village under the Abhaynagar police station, Fultola post office, in Jessore district of

---

[19] Nimai is the other name of Chaitanya Mahaprabhu, a fifteenth-century saint from Bengal, who is believed to be a reincarnation of Krishna. In the song, we hear Sachi Devi's lament, requesting her son not to leave home in order to embrace asceticism.

undivided Bengal. Fultola was a railway station on the Kolkata–Khulna line. Hidiya is three to four miles by boat from Fultola.

Among the different sub-categories within the Namashudras like the Dhani Namoh, Shiuli Namoh, Hele Namoh and Jele Namoh, Sudhamukhi belonged to the Shiuli Namoh Gotra. She writes, 'Hidiya village was home to Muslims, Kayasths, Namashudra (Shiuli and Dhani). There were around four fishermen houses and only one brahmin house. They would celebrate the festivals and rituals, weddings, etc., of all the classes of people.' She further writes,

> My grandfather worked on the farm and my grandmother was a homemaker. In the afternoon, my father would carry my grandfather's lunch to the fields. He had studied up to a level at the village pathshala. In those days, primary education included geometry and measurement. I discovered these texts in a chest after I grew up. My father was married off at the early age of ten to a fellow villager Chandrakanta Roy's youngest daughter (who was then only three years old, her name was Potambori).

Sudhamukhi's official name at school was Soudamini. The panditji at the school registered her under this name when she got admission. This was a school near the village, where the boys went. During that time, palm leaves were used to write upon.

> The palm leaves were stretched out and two of them were tied together. Three or four rings were woven and bound together. This was accompanied by an inkpot and a pen made of bamboo for the purpose of reading and writing. The teacher would first use his nail to cut out the letters on a leaf and then mark them clearly with ink. We used to write the letters by looking at that printed page. In this way, I was promoted to the second year by learning the letters, the different units of measurement (like shatakiya, kora, gonda, pon, ser, katha) and letter writing from the palm leaves.

The second year is when the students moved to paper. After this, there is mention of her education in Classes One and Two. She was married off after this. In the month of Phalgun of the Bengali year 1324, she got married to Banamali Goswami. During the wedding, her name was changed to 'Sudhamukhi'. She was only eight years old.

'During the middle of 1920, I was brought from Hidiya to the Egarokhan area and admitted to Class Three of the school where Shri Goswamiji himself used to teach.' We find the description of the campaign of how she was admitted to the school in Banamali Goswami's *Obor Belar Paari*. Sudhamukhi has described it very briefly:

> There is a village called Banibon near the Uluberia station in Howrah district. There used to be an M. E. school called Baniban Balika Vidyalaya at that place. The school had a concrete, two-storey building. The upper floor was used as a residence for the schoolgirls and the ground floor was used for school work . . . The news that Surodhoni (the wife of Kalidas Biswas) and I had to step outside the village for higher education was not disclosed to anyone except a few young boys. One night Kalibabu sneaked out Surodhoni from her in-law's place and with the help of ten to twelve boys secretly reached Singia station on a boat. From there they took the train to Kolkata and thereafter another train from the Howrah station to reach Baniban, their destination . . . I was supposed to follow next.

In the year 1921, she was admitted to Class Four in Baniban. To reach Baniban, one had to first walk till the Howrah station and then take a train via Uluberia. In 1928, she sat for her Matric exam and alongside it continued her Senior Training. During her four-years stay at the training hostel, she learnt a variety of things. In 1928 these training classes also came to an end and, by the middle of the year, the Matric results were out. She passed both with a second division. Following this, her professional life began.

In 1928, she started working at a Corporation school. By February 1929, she joined the Brahmo Balika Vidyalaya as an assistant teacher. In 1930, she went back to Baniban and joined her old school. She returned to Maliat village in 1931. During this period, Shri Goswami also taught at various schools. Sudhamukhi started teaching at the Prankrishna Balika Vidyalaya at Maliat. There were around 130–140 female students at that time. Among them, 20–25 students used to stay at the boarding house, whose fee was four rupees. The students did not have to pay any fee. Meanwhile, when Shri Goswami went to jail on a case, she provided leadership at the farmers' movement. Later in 1949, Sudhamukhi Goswami took charge as the headmistress of Shimultala Vivekananda Pathshala near Shambhu Nagar in Nadia district. After working at various schools for forty-seven long years from 1928 to 1975, she finally retired. Her daughter, Ms Viva Ghosh Goswami, was elected three or four times from the Nabadwip Lok Sabha constituency and went on to Delhi. Sudhamukhi Goswami passed away on 1 November 2003.

Sushma Maitra Sarkar

Sushma Maitra Sarkar was born in the month of August 1929, in Bethuria, a lesser-known village near Orakandi in the Gopalganj area of Faridpur district. There is a lot of scope for research on Sushma Maitra Sarkar and her work. Around 1944, she completed her IA degree from Ramdiya College. She taught at Shanti Satyabhama Balika Vidyalaya, at the Thakur residence in Orakandi. The collection of stories, essays, poems, plays, biographies authored by her demands being researched as works by a Dalit woman. Just by reading some parts of her writing, we get to know how, through her participation in various events of her time, she mobilised and inspired the girls of her society and Dalit society to come forward.

Her writings have been published in magazines like *Yugantar, Dainik Saptahik, Mashik Basumati, Bharatbarsha,*

Prabashi, Mabatama, Prabartak, Prabhat, Mahila, Meyeder Kagoj, et cetera. Some of the books written by her are *Anya Swad: Anyarong, Ek Ekke Ek, Mahiyashi Shyammohini, Ram Goyalar Swarga Labh, Markin Bidushi Mahila, Bahnni*, and *Mon Mukure*.

Her love for her people and humanity became evident when she wrote,

> The cruel, barbaric tale of the atrocities on the refugees of Morichjhapi—more horrific than the Jallianwala Bagh massacre—was it only to remain a hair-raising story, frozen in the stunned words of Santosh Kumar Mallick: "I saw, I heard, I understood—yet why does the heart remain silent"? So many strings of wounds have been gradually playing in the heart owing to this, leaving it eternally burning in helplessness—this story of merciless torture is also a shameful distorted chapter in the pages of history—we bear the responsibility of writing about it in the correct manner.

Her compassion towards the community shines through when she writes,

> The more I have moved away from the Hindu society (1988) and become a member of free society, I have realised it in each of my senses each day as a follower of Babasaheb Ambedkar that, without any doubt, the caste system will not disappear from Indian society as long as we don't change the religion. Despite knowing that they will be harassed, abused, and condemned at each step for no reason, if someone inflicts extreme cruelty on your soul-relatives and dare to speak to them with glares of insult—I will most definitely protest and deal with them as per my promise to myself as this is my instinctive feeling and I will not tolerate it till I live. However, have I really been able to clear the tag of coward from my name and immerse myself in the chants of revolution? Yet, in the budding pain of my heart I have wished to express that: "jare tumi niche phelo shey tomare badhibe niche" ["they who you push down, will take you to the bottom themselves"]—be aware of these people. By this, I have referred to those people about

ninety per cent of whom came as refugees that day. At this stage, I have not been able to write about the so-called scheduled castes and the Adivasis, especially the others within the scheduled castes like the Poundra, Dhopa, Jele, Muchi, Methor, Kaivarta, Adivasi, and thousands of other castes. In fact, I am writing about a particular community among the so-called scheduled castes, but still many important issues have been left out due to lack of information—like how the treatment of the wound arising from chandsi [piles] has given prominence to a community that specialises in that treatment. In a similar fashion, the names of many teachers, writers, intellectuals, social reformers, politicians, artists, etc., have been left out, ones who have made us proud and brought a sparkle to our eyes.

She has given a call against the caste system in this fashion: 'My feeble writing is an attempt at giving a wake-up call to the race of warriors to rise up in courage at least once instead of staying tied up in the shackled prison of caste. Instead of staying under the effect of being whipped, my feeble attempt comes from the desire to roar out against the perpetrators.'

Let us quote her assessment of Guruchand Thakur from her speech at the festival organised by the Sarbabharatiya Namashudra Samaj Kalyan Parishad on 22 March 1981 at Shantinagar Palta, on the occasion of Guruchand Thakur's 134th birth anniversary.

> Sri Sri Gurchand Thakur welcomed the new age with a new consciousness that began with the establishment of the British Empire in India. He accepted with a generous heart all that is good about Western education. As proof we can look at how by giving space to the Christian missionaries in his village Orakandi, he greatly benefited this community.

Referring to Guruchand's influence on her personal life, she said,

> Had he not founded the Devi Shanti Satyabhama Balika Vidyalaya that day, I would have been deprived of this

opportunity. I completed my education from this very girls' school founded by Sri Sri Guruchand Thakur while living at his house itself and became the first ever and only person to pass the ME scholarship examination by securing first place in the entire Dhaka division, and later got the opportunity to come to Kolkata for my studies.

In 1966-67, she held a conference for all the Scheduled Caste and Adivasi women from Bengal. She also worked for the relief fund that was created for the Bengali refugees of 1971. The Ambedkar Free Primary School near Paik Para was established by her. She left Hinduism and worked to create a free society.

I felt it necessary to talk about these women because history has hardly given them any space. Even if we get to know a little something about Rami Chandidas in the history of Bengali literature, the others have no mention. Sulochona's work is seen in the *Mymensingh Geeti Kobita*, but it has not been mentioned in too many places. Anantabala Vaishnabi was quite a popular artist but not a single one of her records can be found today. Gramophone artist Anantabala had numerous records and rose to the peak of popularity but she remains neglected in history. Royani artist Kamini Bala also gained popularity but she too has been neglected in the history of mainstream Bengali literature and culture. Dalit writer Brajen Mallik's novel *Kolar Mandas* was written with her as the main character. In the case of Sushma Maitra Sarkar, her literary contribution was as significant as her social contribution. However, save for one or two Dalit periodicals, this society showed no obligation to remember her. For these reasons, I feel it is my responsibility to remember them anew to attract the attention of this generation. If at all this can atone for all the neglect!

References

Chaturtha Duniya Patrika - Issue 38.

Goswami, Banamali. *Abar Belar Paari.*

Goswami, Sudhamukhi. *Atmajibonir Moto.*

Haldar, Gopal. *Bangla Sahityer Ruprekha.*

Mallick, Nakul. *Dalit Kantha.*

Roy, Arati. *Satardha Nari.*

Sarkar, Sushma Maitra. *Mon Mukure.*

Sen, Sukumar. *Bangla Sahityer Itihash.*

Sikdar, Nani Gopal (compiler). *Upekkhita Polli Geeti Samraggi Proyata Anantabala Baishnabi.*

Kalyani Thakur Charal – born in Bagula, Nadia district in 1965 – is a prominent voice in Dalit literature. She publishes *Neer Ritupatra*, a platform dedicated to Dalit women's writings. A member of the Bangla Dalit Sahitya Sanstha, she also serves on the editorial board of *Chaturtha Duniya* and is associated with the Dalit Sahitya Academy, Government of West Bengal. She has authored several collections of poetry, short stories, essays, autobiographical writings, and novels. Her notable works include the autobiography *Ami Kano Charal Likhi*, the essay collections *Chandalinir Bibriti 1; 2; 3*, and the edited volume *Matua Dharma Prasange*. She has delivered talks and led workshops on her writings at Monash University, Nottingham Trent University, and SOAS.

Anurima Chanda is an Assistant Professor in the Department of English, Birsa Munda College, University of North Bengal. Her doctoral work was on Indian English children's literature and was awarded her degree from Jawaharlal Nehru University. She was a pre-doctoral DAAD fellow at the University of Würzburg, a SUSI 2023 Fellow at the University of Montana, and was awarded the Charles Wallace 2024–25 Visiting Fellowship at the University of Edinburgh. A literary translator and children's author, her notable works include *How I Became a Writer* (the English translation of Manoranjan Byapari's autobiography; Stree Samya and Sage, 2022), *Bejonma* (a Bengali translation of Sharan Kumar Limbale's autobiography; Doshor, 2022), and *Women of India* (DK Publishing, 2019).